BECOMING A PEOPLE

RE-MEMBERING BLACKNESS IN THE IMAGO DEI

FR. JABRIEL S. BALLENTINE

eBook ISBN-13: 978-1-7373961-1-6

Paperback ISBN-13: 978-1-7373961-0-9

JahBread LLC

Orlando, FL

https://jahbread.com

To all the people created Black by Divine Purpose,

that what was dismembered by White Supremacy might be remembered in you and through you.

The Ethiopic Icon on the cover is a depiction of the Bringing of the
Ark of the Covenant from Jerusalem into Ethiopia, and represents the
moment when the keeping of God's Word shifted from the Hebrews
to the Ethiopians.

Table of Contents

Introduction

It was a long spring day in 2010. I was a student at Howard School of Divinity. After finishing a night class this first day of March, I made my way home to catch my two sons before their bedtime.

It was March 1, 2010 — a Monday. I remember because I didn't make it home that night. You see, I had forgotten that my tags expired at the month's end and that February is a short month, which gave me less time to procrastinate. Who hasn't procrastinated about getting their tags renewed…especially when you're new to "adulting?"

As I get about half a mile from my apartment, the flashing blue lights come to life and I'm stopped by the police. Alright…damn. Maybe I'll get a ticket. I might get away with a warning. I mean…it's only a day beyond expiration.

Moreover (my bourgeois sensibilities kick in), I'm coming home from seminary, dressed in a suit, bow tie, and an elegant fedora. I'm giving the officer all the reasons to assume that I'm the type who procrastinated too long…

Yet, the officers flank my car with their guns drawn: "Get out of the fucking car!"

"I will officer, but would you be kind enough to stop pointing your guns at me?"

"We will once you get out the fucking car!"

After the DC Police grab me from my car at gunpoint, they handcuff me and leave me sitting on the curb while they dig through my car to perform an illegal search of my car's interior and trunk. Once they find nothing, they inform me that my tags are expired, and I was illegally operating a vehicle. They took me to jail.

It was hours before they allowed me to call my then wife and well after midnight before I was able to let her know why I hadn't arrived home from class. Having been arrested for "operating a vehicle illegally," I was denied the opportunity to simply let my family know that I was alive. At 2:00 a.m., I was released with "no paper." No charges were filed, and I was issued a ticket to get my tags renewed which would vacate once my tags were renewed!

I told the desk sergeant (a Black man) upon discharge: "You know y'all could have given me this from the beginning, right?"

He gave me one of those looks and a nod that said, "Yeah…this was some bullshit." I took my stuff and walked the few miles back to my car - which they didn't even impound (thankfully), and finally made it home.

I was held at gunpoint, had my car searched, jailed for hours, denied contact with my family, and released with a warning, to then walk home because my tags were expired by one day!

What did I do?!

I gave thanks to be alive. I gave thanks that it didn't go worse. I gave thanks that I didn't react with indignation at the indignity of the treatment that I received by agents of the State who I pay to protect and serve me.

I updated my tags. I put on the new sticker, and I went on my way. Just another day in Black life…

I allowed the State to take my dignity like my ancestors on plantations who had no choice but to allow Massa, and Massa's agents, to have their way with our person…no choice but to allow Massa to have his way with our wives, our husbands, and our children.

At this point, I imagine you can relate. You can remember the time when you had to suffer an indignity at the hands of those charged to ensure your dignity was not violated. They say the Bill of Rights was necessary to protect the personhood of a free people. Yet, as Black people we have always had to reconcile with the violation of our dignity. We have always had to accept the violation of our dignity. We all have to "shuck and jive" in one sense or another.

That is the root of the problem: an existence that forces us to accept indignities. Everyone should be free to choose when to accept indignity. We, of our own accord, should have the freedom to determine when we think it is best to apply the virtue of humility, or when it might be best to apply the virtue of courage. For when the system has the authority to take that free choice from us and subject us to constant humiliation, what becomes of that "people?"

That "people" would become a "non-people." They would become effectively dehumanized — maybe not fully dehumanized, but dehumanized nonetheless. For how can "a people" be and remain "a people" if that people no longer has the free will to exist and express its essential "being?"

To be Black in America is to deny your free will and to deny the free will of your children. It means teaching your children to subjugate their own dignity, not because that's their choice but because Black children need to learn that if they defend their dignity, they will die.

Does that describe "a people" to you? When you think of a "free people," what is their dignity? What does dignity mean to a free people…for a free people?

I imagine that God would have made some promises to our enslaved ancestors. During slavery, oppression, Jim Crow, and everything that was going on in the fight for freedom, I imagine that God would have made some promises to our enslaved ancestors to give them hope in the midst of hellaciously wicked times.

What do you think?

I imagine that in the height of the first era of lynching in America, God would have made some promises of deliverance that fueled the faithful ones who sacrificed in and for the civil rights movement.

I cannot imagine how we would have overcome such terror and kept hope alive as we've had but for the promises of God. So, what does it mean when God fails to come? As we have witnessed throughout 2020 and for the past few years, we certainly cannot claim to have "come to the place for which our fathers sighed."

In this collection of sermons, we are considering the racial dilemma in America through the lens of Jacob's story. Jacob, the child of Isaac and who's brother, Esau, desired to kill him, represents us Black Americans. We are the sons and daughters of America who, from the birth of this Nation, have been and remain under threat of violence from our White brothers and sisters. Esau represents our White sisters and brothers.

I stumbled upon this understanding when preparing to preach on Jacob as the COVID outbreak commenced. I saw Jacob in a dysfunctional family where his brother was consumed by the desire to kill him and the authorities - his parents - could do and would do nothing to prevent the fratricide.

In addition to allowing Esau to seek opportunities to kill Jacob, Isaac — one of the forefathers of the Faith — continued to prefer Esau. Although Esau had zero regard for the faith of his father, his father still preferred him over Jacob. Isaac still honored Esau as the firstborn who was secured in the privilege of the firstborn.

In this dysfunctional American family, Esau - White America - continues to harbor a desire to kill Black life. White America still harbors a comfort with the systemic killing of Black life and those who stand in the shoes of the Founding Fathers (and Mothers) of America — the Federal Government in its civic trinity of Three Branches — still prefer Esau over Jacob. America still thinks the hope and future for "securing the blessings of Liberty for ourselves and our posterity" rests in White power.

Black power remains subjugated and subordinated to whiteness. Black life remains excluded from the "We the People" enshrined in the Constitution. Black people remain locked out of the blessings of Liberty for our posterity in this Country. The promises have yet to be fulfilled, and we have yet to determine a deadline for their fulfillment.

However, Jacob, son of Isaac and grandson of Abraham, never rested until he received the promises of God. He was determined to see them in his lifetime. Yet, we have become reconciled to the idea that "it won't happen in our lifetime."

Knowing that he was about to be killed, on the night before his assassination, Dr. King proclaimed in his "Mountaintop Speech" that he "may not get there" with us but that we as a people would get to the promised land. He said that as a man who knew he was about to die. This is like Moses who had been told by the Lord that he would not enter the promised land, but the people he had sacrificed for would get there. Now we, who do not expect an assassin's bullet, are using Dr. King's thematic to justify our acceptance of the gradualism against which Dr. King, himself, railed in his Letter from a Birmingham Jail.

As a result, we have literally agreed to gift this struggle to our children and their children, ad infinitum. We have embraced the gradualist approach that Dr. King rejected and left religiously begging at the seat of White power for them to take their knees off our necks.

Yet, who made the promise to Black people? Who made the promise to Black people that our lives would matter? Who promised to deliver us from slavery and the dehumanizing existence of life under White supremacy? With whom should our biggest quarrel be: with White America? Should we not wrestle with God, or at least with His body (the Church), demanding that He bless us now, even at risk of coming up with a limp?

Where is that spirit that holds to the promises of God? Where is the spirit that demands and expects those promises to be fulfilled no matter how strongly White power objects?

"A people" are those who — as a group — have laid claim to and defend their dignity as beings created in the image of God. Without that spirit, we cannot really consider ourselves "a people." Without a level of dignity that we refuse to allow to be violated, we cannot be "a people." Until we find and establish that line that holds sacred the essential mattering of our Blackness in the image of God, we cannot be a people.

How do we reclaim our standing as a people? How do we find our dignity in the image of God and defend that holy dignity? How should we look at God's dealings with His people to understand who we are?

Back in Lent of 2020, we were just getting used to the COVID outbreak and lockdowns, and I was preaching live sermons on YouTube using the Revised Common Lectionary. The use of a lectionary is important to this work, and I should take time to explain why.

A lectionary is an established and universal system of Scripture readings for appointed dates and seasons in the Liturgical Cycle of the Church. Lectionaries are predominantly used by the Orthodox, Catholic, and Mainline Protestant Churches. With a lectionary system, you (the preacher) do not choose the Scriptures appointed for the day. The Scriptures are chosen for you.

As is custom for the Season of Lent, in preparation for the Feast of the Resurrection, we follow the story of Israel's development. From Genesis through Exodus, we are brought along as they follow and reject God…religiously. Thus, this is what we'll answer in the journey of these sermons: How does the Black American Experience follow the experiences of Israel and *his* establishment as "a people?"

I've always preferred preaching from a lectionary because it helps me to remove myself from the message. It prevents me from "having a point to prove" and finding the Scripture that helps to support my point. Rather, I am forced to mine the Scriptures that have been given to me and identify what the Spirit might say from there.

INTRODUCTION

I'm not criticizing anyone else's approach. Yet, it's important to lay out mine as we start this journey together. I want you to understand that these are not messages where I had an agenda and found Scriptures to support my points. I did not start with a premise of, "How do I write sermons for the Black Lives Matter movement?" I wasn't looking through the Bible for various Scriptures that speak to the mattering of Black life.

Rather, I was simply following the Scripture where it led from week to week. Starting with the lectionary for Lent 2020, I followed the text as prescribed by the Revised Common Lectionary. The added irony to that approach is this: The Revised Common Lectionary is a tool of Mainline Denominations of Western Christianity around the world. It unites White Christianity to literally keep White Christians (and their coloreds) "on the same page." Yet, it is the Revised Common Lectionary that laid out the flow of Scripture passages for our journey.

To that end, you'll notice every "chapter" is simply another expository sermon on the particular passage listed. You don't need to read this with your Bible. To begin each chapter, I have included the Scripture references in full. The focus is the Word, and every chapter begins with the Word so that you can familiarize yourself with the particular passages of Scripture in context with the message that follows.

This is a bit countercultural for the Western mind. We are all tuned in to WIIFM Radio (What's In It For Me). We want the quick fix, but this is no quick fix topic. We've been following the wrong path since "freedom came." There is no quick fix.

Rather, in this collection of sermons we will dig a deep well to find that Living Water which has remained beyond the reach, corrupted and diluted by White Supremacist Christianity. Each sermon stands on its own. Yet, by virtue of their scriptural proximity, they build upon one another and share a common thread. You don't need to read them in order, but you will benefit immensely from reading them in order as we cultivate a narrative for reconnecting Black Mattering to the imago Dei and promises of God unto Black people. My hope in this offering is to help you begin constructing a Christian faith that is built on a foundation of essential mattering, so that you can embrace a faith where the mattering of black life is a foundational principle.

May the Lord bless you with faith, hope, and love in and for your Black self that we might find our way unto His Promised Land!

Chapter One

Genesis 28:10-22

Jacob's Ladder

Now Jacob went out from the Well of Oath and went toward Haran. So he came to a certain place and stayed there all night, because the sun had set. Then he took one of the stones of that place and put it at his head, and he lay down in that place to sleep. Then he dreamed, and behold, a ladder was set up on the earth, and its top reached to heaven; and there the angels of God were ascending and descending on it. So behold, the Lord stood above it and said, "I am the Lord God of Abraham your father and the God of Isaac. Do not fear, the land on which you lie I will give to you and your seed. Also, your seed shall be as the dust of the earth; you shall spread abroad to the west and the east, to the north and the south; and in you and in your seed all the tribes of the earth shall be blessed. Behold, I am with you and will keep you wherever you go, and will bring you back to this land; for I will not leave you until I have done what I have spoken to you."

Then Jacob awoke from his sleep and said, "The Lord is in this place, and I did not know it." So he was afraid and said, "How awesome is this place! This is none other than the house of God, and this is the gate of heaven." Now Jacob rose early in the morning, and took the stone he put at his head, set it up as a pillar, and poured oil on top of it. Thus Jacob called the name of that place Bethel; but the name of that city was Luz previously.

Then Jacob made a vow, saying, "If the Lord God will be with me, and keep me in this way I am going, and give me bread to eat and clothing to put on, and bring me back in safety to my father's house, then the Lord shall be my God. And this stone I set as a pillar shall be God's house to me, and of all You give me I will surely give a tithe to You."

In the Name of the Father, the Son, and of the Holy Spirit — One God! Amen.

Heavenly Father, we give thanks to you for your wisdom which knows no end! We thank you for the examples that you give of faithful living for us to follow! Oh, Heavenly Father, open our eyes to see, open our ears to hear, and open our hearts to receive so that we might walk worthy of the calling to which You have called us and the promises You have given! Amen.

If the Word of God is indeed a balm in Gilead to heal the sin sick soul and to make the wounded whole, and if it is indeed as St. Paul says that all scripture is given by inspiration of God and is profitable for doctrine, for reproof, for correction, for instruction in righteousness, then this passage must also be for our benefit. Additionally, it must be for our benefit in these times…as applicable to these times.

So, we look to Jacob's Ladder for insight — The Ladder of Divine Ascent. Jacob had a vision of how the holy ones access the Kingdom. The angels of God were ascending and descending upon this ladder with the Lord at the foot of the ladder and at the head of the ladder.

The Ladder of Divine Ascent is the way that we access the Kingdom. Jacob had just received a blessing from his father before he left, and he saw a vision of the purpose of life and the point of all blessings and blessedness. The point of all blessings is that you can access the Kingdom by them. Any blessing — to be a blessing — must help you to climb the Ladder of Divine Ascent. If what you think is a blessing does not help you to climb the Holy Ladder, it is not a blessing, right?

So, this vision is shown to Jacob in contrast to his brother, Esau's, perspective of life. Esau's life was focused on this life, on the materials of this life, on the things of this life, and the pleasures of this life. Esau, who sold his birthright for gluttony, was also the one who took wives to assert his independence from his mother and his father by bringing home women who were contentious towards his parents. He did this to affirm that he did not need his parents' approval and that he had no intentions of following their way.

Genesis 26:34-35 reads: "Now when Esau was forty years old, he took as wives Judith the daughter of Beeri the Hittite, and Basemath the daughter of Elon the Hittite. But they were contentious with Isaac and Rebekah."

On this passage of Scripture, St. Chrysostom says:

Then for us to learn the boy's indiscretion in taking brides from races he should not have, it revealed to us that one was from the race of the Hittites, the other from the Hivites. Yet knowing as Esau did the pains taken by the patriarch in giving express orders to his servant to select a bride for Isaac from his own tribe and the fact that their mother Rebekah came from Haran, he should not have set his mind on any such thing. In order, however, to show from the outset the undisciplined character of Esau's behavior, he took those wives before seeking advice. And for us to learn their intractable nature Scripture says, "They were at odds with Isaac and Rebekah." What could be more galling than this antipathy when they were due to show complete respect and not only did not do this but were even prepared for hostility?

St. Chrysostom asked about what could be more galling than this antipathy when they were supposed to show complete respect. Not only did they not do this, but they were also prepared for hostility. How in the world do you bring home people who you know are at odds with the way of life for you, your family, or with the God of our fathers and mothers?

Yet, as if once wasn't enough, Genesis 8:8-9 says that Esau was gratified when he noticed that the daughters of Canaan did not please his father. In addition to the wives that he already had, Esau took the daughter of Ishmael to be his wife. When it was abundantly clear that his choice in wives had displeased his father, Esau chose another wife for the sole purpose of displeasing his father — yet again.

How could such a life be worthy of blessing?

In Genesis 25:30-33 we read:

Esau said to Jacob, "Let me taste this red stew, for I am exhausted." Therefore, his name was called Edom. But Jacob said to Esau, "Sell me your birthright today." Esau replied, "Look, I am about to die. What good then is this birthright to me?" Then Jacob said, "Swear to me today." So, he swore to him and sold his birthright to Jacob.

What use is a blessing to someone who would sell their own birthright? Somehow, Esau was still the son who his father Isaac preferred.

When speaking on Esau's behavior, the Ancient Historian Josephus said that by marrying outside his race, Esau was:

Thereby taking upon himself the authority, and pretending to have dominion over his own marriages, without so much as asking the advice of his father; for Had Isaac been the arbiter, he had not given him leave to marry thus, for he was not pleased with contracting any alliance with the people of that country; but not caring to be uneasy to his son, by commanding him to put these wives away, he resolved to be silent.

Isaac still loved and preferred Esau more than Jacob. Isaac chose to be silent even though he did not approve of the way that Esau chose to live his life.

At this point, Jacob was out in a barren place. His father demonstrated indifference toward him, and Jacob fled because his brother literally wanted to kill him, and his father had done absolutely nothing to stop it.

It is here, in this barren place, where Jacob was shown a vision of the possibility of divine ascent. Rather than seeking the love of a father who was impressed by earthly prowess and earthly conquering, even when accompanied by poor character, Jacob was given a vision of the God and Father of his father, Abraham.

In his vision of the God of his father, Abraham, Jacob's vision emphasized the importance of how much you *are*, not how much you *have*. It stressed the significance of how much you should desire and endeavor to climb the Ladder of Divine Ascent.

If you aspire to ascend the Divine Ladder and to be among the holy ones in the presence of the Holy One, consider these questions:

- How high will you climb on this ladder? Would you stop before you reach the top?

- How high will you aspire to ascend on this ladder versus how much will you seek to amass in the world?

- How many things or monuments can you erect to your prominence and dominance while your earthly father is more concerned about how high you can climb on the spiritual plane?

- How much do you strive to be good and live good rather than simply talking about being and living good?

In his classical text, the *Ladder of Divine Ascent*, St. John Climacus describes this ladder as how we acquire the virtues. Climbing the ladder is the process of becoming the better version of humanity as we were created to be in the beginning.

So, while the world may be concerned for how much you can dominate your enemies, Jacob's vision shows what the Lord cares for: how diligently you endeavor to dominate yourself and your tendency to betray the Lord.

After Jacob left his father and all that he had ever known, Jacob now met his true father and all that he would ever need to know. He was shown a vision of the type of love that he was equipped to pursue. He wasn't equipped to pursue the love that his father was willing to give.

His father, Isaac, was willing to give a love for which Esau was more equipped. Esau had demonstrated a bloodthirsty ability to kill simply for the sake of killing. He had raped, pillaged, and stolen. He had done all kinds of things to disobey his father's wishes while spitefully asserting his independence. Isaac was pleased with that level of love.

Jacob was not equipped to be that person, and he was shown a vision of a love for which he was equipped to pursue. It was a way that was not "kill or be killed," "dog eat dog," and "survival of the fittest." Rather, Jacob was shown a vision where the path to fulfillment rested upon aspiring to the Heights even if it meant leaving what was familiar to him.

Jacob's vision is about that Love Supreme, as Coltrane would say, which is attained and brought into existence by our focus on pleasing the Heavenly Father. We are then brought into it, ascending and descending on this ladder. As above, so below on earth as it is in heaven. This is the existence and what the vision is about. It is about access to this type of loving relationship. The next question to consider is, "Why now?"

Why did God decide to show Jacob the vision at this point? Why is this the point in Jacob's life's journey where he needed this vision?

Jacob had to leave his home and his loved ones. He had to leave all that he knew and all that was familiar. Also, let us not forget that he had to leave because his father, Isaac, never made the situation tenable such that Esau would not want to harm his brother. Rather, Isaac fanned the flames of Esau towards Jacob. Genesis 27:40 states, "By your sword you shall live, And you shall serve your brother; And it shall come to pass, when you become restless, That you shall break his yoke from your neck." This is how Isaac, a father, addressed his son and the beef between his sons.

Jacob found himself in a deserted place when he was shown the vision. He was in a space where he needed comfort, and he needed the strength to continue. Imagine dealing with this in your middle age; Jacob was in his 40s at the time. How would you feel if, at this age, you were told to leave your home and all that you have ever known because it is the only way to keep you safe and your only chance to live? What was the purpose of this vision? Why was Jacob granted the vision of the Divine Ladder?

St. Chrysostom considered it the "extraordinary care" of the loving God. He said:

When he saw [Jacob] consenting to the journey in accordance with his mother's advice, which came out of fear of his brother, and taking to the road like some athlete, with no support from any source, leaving everything instead to help from on high, Christ wanted at the very beginning of the journey to strengthen Jacob's resolve.

It was like a low-paid rookie athlete who leaves everything, not the professionals today who make millions. Yet, from the beginning of Jacob's journey, Christ wanted to strengthen Jacob's resolve with nothing but help from on high. So, He appeared to him with the words:

I am the God of Abraham and Isaac. I have caused the patriarch and your father to experience a great increase of prosperity. So far from being afraid, believe that I am He who fulfilled my promises and will shower on you My care.

Brothers and sisters, here it is Jacob was told to leave his home. He left his home with only a staff. He didn't bring anything for his journey. *He didn't receive reparations.* Rather, he left with nothing but the clothes on his back and the staff in his hand.

What a fall from grace, eh?!

When Jacob lived with his father, Isaac, they had all kinds of lavish arrangements. Isaac was a powerful and wealthy man. With his father, Jacob had an entire bed with multiple pillows. And just like that,

Jacob had to leave his home and all that he knew; he left all his privileges, luxuries, and comforts of life.

He found himself in a desolate and barren place that he felt was void of God. He resolved that God was not there because there was no blessedness in that godforsaken place. All the blessings and accoutrements of life were back home where he left them. God could not be in a place where Jacob would not have access to the luxuries of which he had become accustomed.

In this place of desolation with nothing in his possession, Jacob had a vision which assured him that the promises were true. It reiterated and solidified the promise that he indeed shall be blessed, he and his descendants.

He woke up from his vision and he proclaimed, "Surely, God is in this place, and I did not know it." I'm looking around here, and I swear that there's no way that God can be here. God was back there, and there's no way that God can be here too. Nevertheless, "surely God is in this place, and I did not know it."

The Lord had made a promise to Jacob and Jacob knew that he would be saved so long as he was obedient. Genesis 28:20-22 says:

Then Jacob made a vow, saying, 'If the Lord God will be with me, and keep me in this way I am going, and give me bread to eat and clothing to put on, and bring me back in safety to my father's house, then the Lord shall be my God. And this stone I set as a pillar shall be God's house to me, and of all You give me I will surely give a tithe to You.'

After all of this, Jacob made a vow. He avowed that if the Lord God would be with him on his journey, give him bread and clothing, and bring him back to the safety of his father's house, he would offer a tithe to the Lord from all that the Lord gave him. Also, he remembered the stone that was used as his pillow when he saw the vision from God and declared the stone as a pillar which served as Jacob's house of God.

What else could Jacob do but give a tithe?!

If the Lord was going to take him from that place of desolation and bring him back to a space of immense blessedness…thanks be to God! How could he not give a tithe after he received the promises of the Lord?

So, have we, Black people in America and around the world, abandoned God's promises, or are we following a false God? The reason I ask this, brothers and sisters, is to affirm that we want to be free from the constant threat of death at the hands of our White brothers and sisters, right?

God promised us freedom from dehumanization and degradation. He promised a space where Black lives matter, right?

I mean, think on it. Write it in the margins. Share it out loud to test how it feels and sounds to you. What is the single greatest thing that you would envision God would promise to Black people having suffered the indignities of life in White supremacy and White supremacist systems?

Whatever comes to your mind as God's promises to Black people, would you consider that promise to have been fulfilled? Can you consider the promises of God unto a people stripped of the imago Dei in which the promises are created to be fulfilled while Black life is still of no consequence in the environment where you are to grow and thrive in abundant life? It's becoming increasingly clear that White power has no intentions of relinquishing power so that equality of persons and oneness can exist in humanity as it does in the Godhead.

The perichoretic union identifies the interplay and relationship between the three persons of the Trinity — the Father, the Son, and the Spirit Who Are one. They Are persons unto themselves, yet They Are one in the Godhead. They Are one in essence, three in person, but never mixed nor divided.

Clearly, White power has no intentions of living in a dynamic where there is perichoretic union amongst and between the peoples of humanity.

Around 2015, I remember facilitating a workshop at Virginia theological seminary with my *Racial Heresy* podcast co-host, Fr. Cayce Ramey, a White priest from Virginia, which is important for context. He and I spoke about a model of reconciliation with a simple equation: repentance plus forgiveness equals reconciliation.

This means repentance from White folks and forgiveness from Black folks will produce reconciliation. Of course, there is repentance from Blacks and forgiveness from Whites too, but by and large, White folks need to repent. Black folks need to forgive for there to be reconciliation. When we expounded upon this principle, people said it made sense. One of the seminarians, a White woman asked, "So, now I agree with everything you say, but what happens if White folks fail to repent?"

My response was, "Black people need to be prepared to leave. If there will be no repentance, there can be no reconciliation."

If White power is unwilling to repent, it might be best for us to leave. Reconciliation cannot be achieved if, like Esau, White power is intent on doing harm to Black bodies. Moreover, reconciliation is not possible if those with fatherly authority in this country still prefer:

- the progeny who prospered while betraying every ideal of America's Abraham in the Founding Fathers.

- the sons and daughters of the Confederacy who took up arms against their Mother Country and Founding Fathers.

- those who betrayed the family and the Union, and whose ideals betray the principles for which we claim to stand as a Republic.

It is highly problematic when our country and the elders of our country prefer those children who have murderous intent towards their own American brothers and sisters. This may manifest through the sinful intent found in the vitriolic violence of police brutality and vigilante killings or the murderous intent rooted in the genteel manifestations of red lining, gerrymandering, and policies that create disparities across all aspects of social living. It could also be that our country and elders' appeal to gradualism bears witness to a society with an ability to tolerate and abide the reality of suffering being experienced by their brothers and sisters.

If our American "fathers" prefer White America's Esau to Black America's Jacob, how else can we be free from the constant threat of death at the hands of our White sisters and brothers, except we consider Rebecca's advice to Jacob and withdraw from this place until our brothers and sisters' wrath has turned away from us? That's what Rebecca said. Rebecca turned to her son, and she said, "Hey, your brother is going to kill you. It might be best for you to leave this place until your brother calms down and stops wanting to kill you!"

The problem is that we are afraid to leave this land of mythical prosperity to go off to a land that we think is desolate.

In 2020, the trumpet sounded for Brother C.T. Vivian. May the Lord be gracious to favorably receive his testimony!

In Vivian's book *Black Power and the American Myth*, he challenged the assertions of American exceptionalism and the mythology of America. In the book, he stated that when they engaged the civil rights movement, they engaged from a framework of looking at how every other group of people got their rights in this country. Others got their rights by banding together and asserting themselves. The Irish, Italians, and Germans all got their rights that way, as did many others. Everybody who got their rights all say that when they came to this country, they weren't received at first. Then, they had to make "a way" by banding together as a people and demanding that America include them in this exceptional society.

That's the premise with which they went into the movement. It became clear, by the witness of the movement, that when Black power is applied to the American system, all the ideals of America proved to be mythological. Somehow, the "truths" about American Democracy and the system that allows the people to protect their lives and liberty from tyranny by the State or the populous all fall apart when Black power does what any other group has done to assert their mattering and "secure the Blessings of Liberty to (themselves) and (their) Posterity." The promises of America, unto Black America, have continuously proven to be lies at worst and gross exaggerations at best. Yet, we are afraid to leave this land.

We are afraid to leave this land of mythical prosperity for a land that we think is desolate. We won't call them "shithole countries" like Donald Trump, but that's what we think. Most of us won't even say that it's fear; you know that we'll choose to be indignant. We express sentiments like, "Why should I leave? My people built this country" …and we did.

We not only built this country from the free labor of the enslaved but also from the free sacrifice of men like Crispus Attucks and Alexander Hamilton. Yes, Alexander Hamilton, a Black man from Nevis, West Indies raised on the island of St. Croix in the United States colony of the Virgin Islands. There were many others who we do not know whose free sacrifices helped build this country. We built America…just like Jacob helped to build up his father's land.

Still, some of us will get indignant. We bitterly proclaim, "I ain't no African; I ain't never been there, and why would I go there?"

When will be the time for us to consider the option of Exodus? Who is considering the life of Abraham who left his home in old age to make a new life in a strange place? Who is considering Jacob, who fled a brother with murderous intent to find the place where God was honored, and beloved community really had a chance to thrive?

God promised deliverance to our ancestors and a home where we would be welcomed and valued in a place where our Black lives matter. Don't get me wrong. I can't point out where He said that, but for God to be a loving God, wouldn't that be part of His promise? Doesn't that have to be the type of thing that He would say for Him to be who we claim that He is?

We didn't always think that our home would be in this country. That's actually a fairly recent development. It was a development spawned by Frederick Douglass and his ilk. Before then, our thoughts were geared towards leaving here.

It's the ideological origins of Black nationalism. When you look at Vessey, Turner, Blyden, and Hubert Harrison, their angle was emigration — exodus. However, our perspective changed, and our eyes became focused on remaining in Egypt.

We began to believe that we could show and prove ourselves to White society. We thought our faithfulness would prove us to be worthy of their love, affection, and adoration as well as their brotherhood and sisterhood in the American family. We came to believe that if we just put our heads down and accept our place, we would show them that we are worthy of their blessing and acceptance, and that they should stop killing us.

We are still asking them to stop killing us. So, the reality is that after over 150 years, assimilation and integration have proven to be failed solutions. We are still wandering in the wilderness while the Israelites were only in the wilderness for 40 years. We are still languishing in the wilderness following leadership that keeps us returning to Egypt, the land of our oppression, looking to them for our freedom.

What if we held the position that either a) the God Who promised freedom to our ancestors is faithful to His promises, and we have given up faith in His promises or b) that our conception of God is false, and we need to realign our faith?

I'm saying to you, brothers and sisters, that it must be an either/or; there is no in-between. Either God is faithful to His promises, no word will come back to Him empty, and it will do what He has purposed for it to do. Either God is faithful, and we are the ones who are unfaithful, or we are following the wrong god who is not a god.

Why would the God Who is faithful allow our situation to worsen if we are indeed faithful to Him and the pursuit of His promises? What hope can we have if we are indeed pursuing the fulfillment of promises that He made to our people, but He has yet to fulfill them? Do we believe God is watching us walk worthy of His call and allowing us to languish under White tyranny for "kicks and giggles?"

What kind of holy sadism is that?

It must be one or the other. Either God is faithful, and we are failing to align with Him, or we are faithful, and doing what is right in our journey toward the promised land, and the "god" that we are following is not able to deliver.

So, what do you believe?

Is it that God is faithful, and we need to realign ourselves because we have been going the wrong way? Or, are we doing what we are supposed to be doing, and it's just that God is not faithful? Could it be that we are following the wrong "god" — who is not God?

I believe that God is faithful, and that we are out of alignment. I refuse to believe that God is not faithful. It's not possible that we have been doing as we should be doing, but God wants us to be here in this condition. I refuse to believe that He's an unaffectionate sadist who is watching us suffer in misery. I believe that the opposite is true. There is hope in knowing that while we are out of alignment, God is still faithful.

To believe that God is faithful, remains faithful, always has been faithful, and always will be faithful and that we are out of alignment is hopeful because all we then have to do is realign with God. To believe that God has, is, and always will be faithful gives us hope because this means that we simply need to realign ourselves with God.

In your opinion, what is the single greatest thing that we need to do to realign ourselves with the God Who alone is able to save?

This is a critically important question. The Israelites wandered in the wilderness for 40 years, and it seems like we cycle through similar traumatic experiences every 40 or 50 years.

First, it was slavery. Then, 40 to 50 years after the end of plantation slavery, the era of lynching erupted, then came the civil rights movement of the sixties. Now, there's the Black Lives Matter movement.

We're just circling around in the wilderness coming to the same point every time. We must align with God. A good example of alignment is the disciples who were in the upper room waiting on the Holy Spirit after the resurrection of Jesus. They had been shaken by the crucifixion of our Lord, yet once they were realigned, the Holy Spirit rushed into the room like a mighty wind.

Instantly, all of them were able to proclaim His glory in the languages of the people around them. As you can see, the Lord takes no time when He is determined. Still, He takes time for you and me to get in alignment. Thanks be God.

So, let us get in alignment and set our eyes on the beloved community. We must stop trying to make beloved community where that beloved community is being rejected. The Lord gives you strength and courage. The Lord make his face to shine upon you. The Lord lift up his countenance on you and give you peace. In the Name of the Father, Son, and Holy Spirit — One God! Amen.

Chapter Two

Genesis 29:1-28

Jacob and Rachel

Now Jacob went on his journey and came to the land of the east, to Laban. So he looked and saw a well in the field; and behold, there were three flocks of sheep lying by it, for out of that well they watered the flocks; and a large stone was on the well's mouth. Now all the flocks would be gathered there; and they would roll the stone from the well's mouth, water the sheep, and put the stone back in its place on the well's mouth. So Jacob said to them, "My brethren, where are you from?" And they said, "We are from Haran." Then he said to them, "Do you know Laban the son of Nahor?" And they said, "We know him." So he said to them, "Is he well?" They said, "He is well. Look, his daughter Rachel is coming with the sheep." Then he said, "It is still high day; it is not time for the cattle to be gathered together. Water the sheep, and go and feed them." But they said, "We cannot, until all the shepherds are gathered together, and they have rolled the stone from the well's mouth; then we will water the sheep." Now while he was still speaking with them, Rachel came with her father's sheep, for she was a shepherdess. And it came to pass, when Jacob saw Rachel the daughter of Laban, his mother's brother, and the sheep of Laban, his mother's brother, Jacob went near and rolled the stone from the well's mouth, and watered the flock of Laban, his mother's brother. Then Jacob kissed Rachel, and lifted up his voice and wept. So Jacob told Rachel he was her father's relative and

Rebekah's son, and she ran and told her father these words. Then it came to pass, when Laban heard the report about Jacob, his sister's son, that he ran to meet him, and embraced him and kissed him, and brought him to his house. So he told Laban all these things. Now Laban said to him, "Surely you are my bone and my flesh." And he stayed with him for a month. Then Laban said to Jacob, "Because you are my brother, should you therefore serve me for nothing? Tell me, what should your wages be?" Now Laban had two daughters: the name of the elder was Leah, and the name of the younger was Rachel. Leah's eyes were delicate, but Rachel was beautiful in form and appearance. Now Jacob loved Rachel; so he said, "I will serve you seven years for Rachel your younger daughter." So Laban said, "It is better that I give her to you than to another man. Stay with me." So Jacob served seven years for Rachel, and they seemed only a few days to him because of the love he had for her. Then Jacob said to Laban, "Give me my wife, for my days are fulfilled, that I may go in to her." Now Laban gathered together all the men of the place and made a wedding feast. Thus it came to pass in the evening, he took Leah his daughter and brought her to Jacob; and he went in to her. So Laban gave his maid Zilpah to his daughter Leah as a handmaiden. Then it came to pass in the morning, behold, it was Leah; and he said to Laban, "What is this you have done to me? Was it not for Rachel that I served you? Why then have you deceived me?" Laban replied, "It must not be done so in our country, to give the younger before the firstborn. Fulfill her week, and I will give you this one also for the service you will render me still another seven years." Then Jacob did so and fulfilled her week. So he gave him his daughter Rachel as wife also.

In the Name of the Father, the Son, and the Holy Spirit — One God! Amen.

Father, we give thanks to You for the grace of life. We give thanks to You who give us the way to live. Help us, oh Lord and give us the strength and courage in the midst of deceit, hatred, and envy. Help us to remain true to Your promise and to remain faithful to our first love that we might walk worthy of the calling to which we have been called. Amen!

We are back to following the life and exploits of Jacob. We've been journeying with Jacob through the Black Experience and journeying as Black people through the story of Jacob's experience. If you remember in the previous chapter, we were with Jacob as he usurped his brother Esau's birthright. Esau didn't care for his birthright. He had no regard or use for it. All he wanted to do was live lavishly. He was caught up in material living. Esau cared only for prosperity in his present life. To demonstrate his penchant for exploitation, he was willing to give his birthright to his brother, Jacob, for a plate of food. He didn't want to cook for himself. He essentially told Jacob, "Hey, I'll give you my birthright! I'm hungry, man. Give me this food!"

Esau sold his birthright to his brother, Jacob. Jacob went to lay claim to that birthright and to procure the blessing from his father, Isaac. Yes, Jacob was deceitful in getting the blessing from his father, and as a result, his brother wanted to kill him. So, Jacob fled. Have you ever heard of a brother killing his own brother? This is similar to Cain who slew Able.

Esau wanted to kill Jacob, and the real problem was that no one could stop Esau. His father couldn't stop him. His mother — their mother — couldn't stop Esau from his murderous intent. The best thing that they could do was to send Jacob away. "You have to run because your brother is going to kill you!"

Jacob ran from this brother, with murderous intent, and all he had was a staff to his name. He had no possessions and when he laid down to sleep that night, all he had was a rock stone for his pillow. If you remember, while sleeping on that rock stone, he saw a vision of a Divine Ladder reaching into the heavens with the angels of God ascending and descending upon it. The Lord was at both the foot and head of the ladder comforting Jacob saying, "I will be with you. I am your God. Don't worry about what's going on right now. I am making a promise to you that you will have life and have life in abundance."

Then, Jacob realized, "Man, I thought I was in desolation. I just left the place where I knew God was. I just knew that this place was void of any goodness, no hope, and without God. I didn't have any hope of possessing this abundant life after my parents urged me to flee and search elsewhere for it. Surely, the Lord is in this place, and I did not know it! Now I have hope for life! I can do this!"

After seeing the vision, Jacob was like, "Man, if you do these things for me, Lord, You will be my God." He bargained, "You will be my God. I will obey You. I will follow You. I will give thanks to You. What's more, out of everything that You give me, I will tithe to You too. Thanks be to You!"

Well, he didn't say it in those words, but if you read it, that's what he said.

Now we are caught up to the Scripture that grounds this message from the life and exploits of Jacob: Genesis 29:1-28. If you read these things, you see some crazy stuff. I tell people: if you like soap operas, you'll love the Old Testament because it's a debauchery! What treachery! What deception! They lie, cheat, and steal; there's all kinds of nonsense! We're supposed to be discussing a righteous story in the developments of holiness, and we're talking about this kind of stuff, right?

In our society, we've moved beyond the dowry, but the dowry was a part of Jacob's time and culture. So, ignore any of your thoughts on whether or not a dowry is a "right" thing. Settle on this simple reality: Jacob and Laban made a deal, and Jacob was clear. I can hear Jacob now, "I want your younger daughter, and you wait until after the seven years of our agreement to tell me that the agreement is incomplete because your culture requires that the first born is given away first?! You didn't say that when we made the deal! You didn't say, 'We don't do it that way here. Here, the firstborn must go first.' I could have decided ahead of time if I wanted to serve you for the firstborn and then serve you again for the younger daughter, who I prefer. You let me think that we had an honest deal. Then when I do my part, you move the goal posts and change the deal."

So, Jacob really served another seven years? Can you imagine how Jacob must have felt? Put yourself in his position. Don't mind whatever objections you would have to the very nature of the whole story. Just put yourself in that position and imagine how he must have felt. Imagine he said, "I just served you these seven years. I just gave you seven years of my life. I didn't have anything. You know I came with nothing but my staff. If I had money, I would have simply paid the dowry for your daughter, but I gave you seven years of my life. (It was more wages than what would have been paid for a woman in those times — almost double the going rate.) I gave you all this service, and this is how you treat me? Now I'm supposed to serve you for another seven years and trust you again?"

It all goes back to Jacob's entrance into Haran. He was thrown out of his home and away from all that he knew. His life was turned upside down and everything changed. He had gone from a person of privilege, living in his father's house with many amenities, to being a man in squalor where a rock stone was his pillow.

By the grace of God, he had a vision telling him about blessings beyond measure. "Don't worry," says the Lord. "Don't fret. Don't fear. You're going to be blessed."

"Okay, cool," I hear Jacob say. "Surely the Lord is in this place. I have a little strength now and a little comfort from the Lord to move forward in this journey towards the promised land. You've made Your promises to me, Lord, okay? I will hold you to them by doing my part. Since You are calling to me from atop the Divine Ladder, I will walk worthy of the calling to which I have been called. Let's see if you're going to be the God that You have said You are because if I do my part, surely you will do yours."

Later, he moved forward from that place and went to his motherland which was the land of Haran where his mother told him to go find a bride. Here, we understand that when we are talking about establishing a nation and a people, you must have a bride! You can give me all the riches in the world, but if I died without a bride with whom to have something progeny, the nation dies with me.

Therefore, it started with Jacob's quest to find a bride. To receive this blessedness that the Lord had promised Jacob, he had to first identify his bride.

He walked into the city and started to execute his mission. Did they know Laban? Yes, and Laban still lived there. Was he well? Yes, he was alive and well and his daughter was near him! That's how well he was doing. He saw how beautiful Rachel, Laban's daughter, was. When he saw her, it was like Adam coming out of his trance to see Eve for the first time: "This is now flesh of my flesh and bone of my bones!" It was love at first sight.

He saw Rachel and instantly, he became a believer! Many men have seen a woman and became a believer in higher things! Really, when the right potential mate comes along, you become a believer, right?

It blessed Jacob tremendously to see the woman who he had been promised to find, and he tried to impress her. All the men were waiting for others to come help move the stone that was in front of the well so that they could water the sheep.

If you look at the Word, the men said they could not water the sheep until all the shepherds gathered to roll the stone from the well's mouth. Jacob said, "I don't need all the shepherds to come. I am going to show her my machismo. I will move this stone by myself." Then, he moved the stone from in front of the well. I can imagine that he stood up tall to flex his muscles for her.

It was love at first sight. After he moved his stone, he walked over and kissed Rachel. Brothers and sisters, she was the assurance of the promise of God.

Jacob had just been promised that he would have a prosperous existence if he trusted the Lord to deliver him. Again, at that time, he could not have a prosperous existence without a wife...without offspring. Now, imagine what Rachel must have meant to him.

What Rachel and the fulfillment of God's promise meant to Jacob is demonstrated by his willingness to serve another seven years with this man who had just deceived him. The promise of God was wrapped up in Rachel, and that promise had to be fulfilled.

In his lived response, it's as if Jacob is saying, "When I was at the lowest point, in that desolate place, You came to me, Lord, and told me about this promise. That promise is what made me get up from this place with hope to carry on, so that promise must be fulfilled!"

He committed himself to see this through and to give this God a fair shot. "I am going to give you a fair shot, Lord. I won't expect you to just wave a magic wand and make everything good for me. I will give you a fair shot by enduring injustice and not being deterred from my first love."

Brothers and sisters, we want to see the promises of God fulfilled in our lives, right? We want to see the promises of God fulfilled in our lifetime, right? Do you want whatever God promised in this life to come when you are gone?

We want the promises of God that were meant for us to be fulfilled in our lives and in our lifetime. My Black brothers and sisters, how would you describe the promises that were made for us — in freedom from slavery, the ending of Jim Crow and the lynching era, during the nadir of America and race relations, segregation, and Black codes? What do you believe about these promises that were made to our ancestors for them to come to believe God to be good all the time and all the time, for Him to be good? How would you identify or describe what those promises would be?

If you stop and think about our great God, what do you imagine the promises of God are for us based on the relationship between Him and the people he chose as an example of His love for us in His Holy Book? What does that look like? Paint that picture. What do you see?

The problem is that we have compromised our commitment to God's promise to satisfy ourselves with Leah. We accept our present reality as if it were somehow part of the original deal for which our ancestors died. We accept this existence as if it could ever be any part of the promise of God. What part of the promise of God could this be?

Do you really believe that our social condition in these times is somehow part of God's promise? It might be on the path to fulfillment, but it surely cannot be the place where we rest and stay. We must not become reconciled to the injustice, betrayal, or deceit of Laban by allowing that injustice to become part of our vision for and understanding of God's promises for us.

It would be as if Laban said: "You know what? After these seven years of service, I'm not giving you Rachel. I'm going to give you Leah." Then Jacob responds, "Okay. I give you the authority to call an audible on God's promise for me. I will reconcile myself to Leah and be happy because you are right, Laban. This is what God wants for me. You know best and thank you for moving the goalpost. I would be worse off if you hadn't deceived me!"

Because we are satisfied with Leah, we can't even conceive of what God's promises might be. We must think about it and dig deep. We must remember our first love. Remember the vision of the promise. We must reconnect with what that promise must have been.

Again, not just words of the promise but the embodiment of that promise. For Jacob, Rachel was the embodiment of the promise of the Lord. She was beautiful in form and appearance.

"This is the promise! I see you, Lord! I see it, and I give thanks to You, Lord." This is why Jacob kissed her and lifted up his voice: "Thanks be to God! I see it Lord! This is the embodiment of the promise right here. What should separate us from the love of God? Shall the deception of Laban separate us?" Shall whatever White power wants to do separate us?! What shall separate us from our first love?! Nothing!

We must remember our first love — what she looked like, what she smelled like, and what it was like when we first laid eyes on her. We must remember why we were willing and able to go through hell and high water to receive her. Brothers and sisters, you must get a picture of what that promise would look like in your mind's eye...in your third eye.

When you close your eyes and you look deep within the recesses of the self and your soul, what does the promise of God for us look like to you? How might it be embodied? How do you see it? Where do you see it? How do you envision it? Get a picture of what the promise of God for us must look like for God to be good and hold firm to that picture so that you remember your first love. Then, beloved, we must set our heart's intention to be joined to our first love—to be joined to the embodiment of that promise, the beloved community, and the place where Black lives matter which is beautiful like Rachel, in form and appearance. The promise of God dwells in that beloved community where love abides and where mattering is a given because we are created in the imago Dei.

Beloved, we used to sing, "Keep your eyes on the prize. Hold on." However, we must remember which prize is the prize! Which prize have we been keeping our eyes on? Have we been keeping our eyes on Leah as the prize who was the product of Laban's deception, or do we keep our eyes on the prize that was revealed to us in the promises of God?

Don't get me wrong, do right by Leah because the betrayal and the deception were not Leah's fault. Do right by the people, places, and things that you've had and have as long as the deception and betrayal was not the fault of those people, places, and things. Still, do not settle for the vision that was crafted for you by the Labans of America. Do not reconcile yourselves to their vision of God's promise for your life and freedom from their oppression. Keep your eyes on the prize. Hold on and remember your first love.

So how do we do this? What do you do? First, we must identify and remember our first love. That means identify the embodiment of God's promises to us as a people who are free from the dehumanizing experience and legacy of chattel slavery, Jim Crow, mass incarceration, and the myriad other social ills of White supremacy.

How do you identify the embodiment of God's promises to us as a people? What does it look like? What could it possibly be? What could God have possibly been promising to us? What would be the promise of God to his people who have been subjected to such atrocities? How do you envision that promise being made manifest?

Once Jacob had the vision of the Ladder, erected the pillar, and went into the city, he believed that promise would be made manifest. He took the Lord at His Word. He expected that vision to be made manifest in his lifetime and not sometime in the distant future, for some people didn't remember Jacob nor the making of the promise.

How would you envision the promise of God to our people be made manifest in your lifetime? After you've identified and created a picture in your mind's eye of your first love, what would need to happen in the next four to six months for you to become more faithful and realign your life with the fulfillment of that promise?

Jacob was faithful to the promise because it had to be fulfilled. He still saw Rachel as the embodiment of the promise. Laban may have deceived him, placed obstacles in his way, took advantage of him, and got the better of him. Yet, nothing would sway Jacob from pursuing the fulfillment of God's promise. Jacob would not allow anything to deter or distract him from a clear vision of the promise. He was faithful. He endured. Whatever came his way, he had to endure.

Jacob resolved, "Okay. I must endure this. I've been deceived? Okay, cool. I'll endure this, and we'll keep going toward the promise. I have to serve Laban even longer? Okay. I'll endure, but I'm going to keep going forward toward the promise. I will live faithful to that promise. I won't betray that promise. I won't turn away from that promise. I won't reshape that promise into something that makes me more comfortable in the now. I'm going to be faithful to that promise, Lord, and make You show Yourself approved the same way I must show myself approved. In mutuality, in oneness, and in tewahedo, we will do this together, Lord. I will, with God's help!"

What would you have to do to start living your life as if you believed that the promise of God was going to be fulfilled in your life in your lifetime?

Jacob didn't wait for his descendants' lifetime. It might have taken seven extra years. It might have taken an extra six years after that. In his lifetime, he became more than a conqueror. He had conquered the temptations to abandon the promises of God. He had conquered the various reasons for abandoning the promises of God. He had conquered the reasons to lose hope and changed his perspective on the promises of God. He was more than a conqueror because he remained faithful to the promise. No matter what trial or tribulation came his way, nothing separated him from the love of God in Jesus Christ.

Paul asked, "What shall separate us from the love of God?" Shall trials? Shall tribulations? Shall injustice? Shall unfairness? What shall separate us from the love of God?

I am sure that none of it shall separate us from His love. For we will embrace His love, come what may! Regardless of what Babylon might try to do to prevent us and sway us from pursuing his love, we will remain faithful to His promise. Identify and remember your first love and stay faithful. Know that God's promises must be fulfilled as long as we are faithful to his call.

May the Lord give you strength and courage to stay faithful to His call! May you persevere and give Him the opportunity to show His faithfulness and expect His deliverance that we might ascend to the heights of the beloved community and live in this life on earth, as it is in Heaven. May the blessing of God Almighty, the Father, the Son, and the Holy Spirit guide, protect, keep, and strengthen you from this day forth and evermore! Amen!

Chapter Three

Genesis 32:22-32

Jacob's Ladder

Now Jacob went out from the Well of Oath and went toward Haran. So he came to a certain place and stayed there all night, because the sun had set. Then he took one of the stones of that place and put it at his head, and he lay down in that place to sleep. Then he dreamed, and behold, a ladder was set up on the earth, and its top reached to heaven; and there the angels of God were ascending and descending on it. So behold, the Lord stood above it and said, "I am the Lord God of Abraham your father and the God of Isaac. Do not fear, the land on which you lie I will give to you and your seed. Also, your seed shall be as the dust of the earth; you shall spread abroad to the west and the east, to the north and the south; and in you and in your seed all the tribes of the earth shall be blessed. Behold, I am with you and will keep you wherever you go, and will bring you back to this land; for I will not leave you until I have done what I have spoken to you."

Then Jacob awoke from his sleep and said, "The Lord is in this place, and I did not know it." So he was afraid and said, "How awesome is this place! This is none other than the house of God, and this is the gate of heaven." Now Jacob rose early in the morning, and took the stone he put at his head, set it up as a pillar, and poured oil on top of it. Thus Jacob called the name of that place Bethel; but the name of that city was Luz previously.

Then Jacob made a vow, saying, "If the Lord God will be with me, and keep me in this way I am going, and give me bread to eat and clothing to put on, and bring me back in safety to my father's house, then the Lord shall be my God. And this stone I set as a pillar shall be God's house to me, and of all You give me I will surely give a tithe to You."

In the Name of the Father, the Son, and the Holy Spirit — One God! Amen!

Heavenly Father, we give thanks to You for the life that you have given unto us for you, indeed, have created us in Your image and made us promises! We give thanks to You for being a God Who is always sure to fulfill His promises to us! Amen. Oh Lord, give us strength and give us courage! Give us hope that we might remember your promises and that we might walk worthy of your promises, trusting in their fulfillment! Amen!

In this passage, Jacob has returned to his fatherland and had another encounter with his murderous brother, Esau. Jacob was on his way back to Isaac's land where Esau had never left. Jacob knew that he was about to encounter his brother after he fled his motherland.

As Black people, I want us to think about this notion of the fatherland and the motherland. We can see the fatherland as the land where Esau was. It is the land we had to flee because of our murderous brother. Our motherland is the land where we thought we would find safety.

Jacob returned to his fatherland, the land of oppression. He had to flee the motherland because his murderous uncle Laban was creating problems. Jacob was on the run again.

Yes, Jacob had prospered much — so much that he had two wives! Lord have mercy! He had tons of cattle. He had an entourage at his beck and call. He had prospered in the land where he was. He had risen to seats of power (like the Black bourgeoisie of our time) yet, he was still without a home. He had no place to rest his head. Just like when he was on that rock stone for his pillow, he had no place to rest his head. He was still unwanted and unwelcome.

Jacob prepared to encounter his brother, Esau. He returned to his fatherland because the Lord appeared to him and told him to return to his father, Isaac. And when he laid on that rock stone and had the vision of the Divine Ladder, he promised to obey the Lord.

There he was, knowing that he was about to encounter his murderous brother again, but he wasn't sure if he would be well-received or met with the traditional vitriol that came from encounters with Esau. He prepared to go back to his fatherland and with everything in order, Jacob decided to split his camp in two. He sent his wives ahead of him in different directions. He determined that if Esau killed one half, at least the other half could escape and some of his family could be spared.

Jacob sent his servants ahead of him with gifts of livestock, cattle, and other things. Each servant proclaimed, "My master, Jacob, has sent this for you and more is coming behind me." That night, before Jacob went to see his brother Esau, Jacob was alone, and he wrestled with God. This is where we begin in Genesis 32:22-32.

Why in the world would Jacob wrestle with God? Is that not the question to be asked?

Yes…the text says, "a Man," but tradition has always taught that it is God Who Jacob wrestled. Why in the world would Jacob wrestle with God?! Imagine the Lord coming to you, and then imagine that rather than falling to worship Him, you square off and prepare for fisticuffs?

Surely, there were many options that Jacob could have chosen as the focus of his fight. There was Laban who had wronged him repeatedly over the span of 20 years. There was Esau, who ran Jacob off in the first place and desired to kill Jacob because Esau wanted to go back on his word about giving Jacob his birthright. There was Jacob's mother who sent him to Laban. Did she not know that her brother was a cheat?

His mother was unable to find another way to protect Jacob from Esau without sending her "favorite son" away. There was also Jacob's father who preferred Esau over Jacob in the first place, even though Esau had complete disregard for the way established by Abraham.

All these people had betrayed him at one point or another. All these people had shortchanged and misled him, but those people were fallible. They were all human, and we know what we say about the failings of humanity. With them, Jacob could be as cunning as a serpent yet harmless as a dove…and he was.

Jacob was able to procure the promise birthright that Esau wanted to deny. He and Esau made a deal. Esau wanted to renege on the deal. Jacob was able to procure the birthright despite Esau's intention to break his deal. He would not be denied what was promised to him.

He was able to get the promised wife. No one was gonna deny him Rachel. He was able to get the promised cattle with which to start life on his own. Laban wanted to change the arrangement all the time, but Jacob was able to get the better of him and procure the desired cattle upon which they had agreed.

Jacob was able to extract the promises from those earthly beings who had made promises to him. They did not want to fulfill the promises they had made to Jacob. They made those promises with no expectation of Jacob ever receiving what was promised. Although there was no intention of fulfilling the promises made to Jacob, he faithfully pursued the promise of God, even before he had truly met God.

Jacob did not allow the whims of those fallible beings to thwart his trust in and pursuit of the promises of God. No matter what those fallible human beings did, he was not going to allow that to cause him to doubt that the promises of God would be fulfilled in his lifetime. The only other being associated with these promises and who had yet to fulfill a promise to Jacob was God.

Being brought face to face again with the brother he had previously outsmarted, Jacob was clearly still on the run. This "god" had promised him this land. God had told Jacob this land would be a place where his family could rest, grow, and multiply. As he prepared to face his brother again, Jacob needed to know Emmanuel — that God was with him.

Jacob chose to direct his fight toward the God Who had promised and not yet fulfilled. He wasn't about to let God go until He had given Jacob blessed assurance that the holy promise was his. Back in Genesis 28:13-15, the Lord had promised that He would not leave Jacob until He had fulfilled His promise saying, "I will not leave you until what I have spoken has come to pass."

When Jacob wrestled with God, the Lord made himself manifest for Jacob to seek. He and Jacob wrestled all night long. At daybreak,

God wanted to return to obscurity and Jacob refused to let the Lord leave without blessing him. That's what the Lord wants us to see, brothers and sisters.

Amid the turmoil that we endure in this western world, especially America, and this uprising for the mattering of Black lives, we want a space where Black lives matter — not that Black lives matter more than anybody else's. I know that people use the term "Black lives matter" as a declarative statement, but that cry isn't really declaring that Black lives matter. It's a cry yearning for Black lives to matter in the midst of a space that is telling them that Black lives do not matter.

What we want is a space where Black lives matter — where Ham, Shem, and Japheth can at last live in love, right? So yes, we want a place where all lives matter because Black lives matter.

What do you envision? What do you want while in this turmoil? What do you envision are the promises of God to our people? We need to get comfortable imagining and articulating the promises of God for us as a people. Words have power, brothers and sisters, so let us speak life!

I imagine such would have been the promise of God to our ancestors and elders, to those who suffered under chattel slavery and all other heinous acts of White supremacy, both vitriolic and genteel. I imagine that God would have promised to our ancestors and to our elders a place where we would not have to question our value. I imagine a place where we would not have to struggle to matter (a basic thing of life), but to matter simply because all lives truly do matter.

Brothers and sisters in Christ, I cannot imagine a promise of God to our people that would involve us still begging to matter. The problem is that we are not determined to see those promises fulfilled in our lifetime. We say that we believe the promises and that we want to see them. Oh yeah! If we are asked, "Do you believe in the promises of God unto our people?", we will all say, "Yeah! I believe in the promises!" If I ask, "Do you want to see these promises fulfilled?" All will say, "Oh yes, I want to see them fulfilled!"

Nevertheless, we've already reconciled ourselves to dying beyond the Gates of the Promised Land. "I may not get there with you." We say it all the time. We inculcate it. We teach it. We pay it forward. We bequeath it to our progeny. We teach it to our children and their children.

It won't happen in our lifetime.

We condition ourselves to struggle just for the sake of struggle. That's what we're supposed to do as Black people in America — struggle. If you don't struggle, you're not a good Black person, and so we struggle.

To where are we struggling? I don't know, but we "keep calm & struggle on" because that's what good Black people do. Sadly, we no longer have a determination to see the promises of God fulfilled in our lifetime.

Brothers and sisters, the life of Jacob and his experience wrestling with God provide guidance for how we ought to remain faithful to the promises that were made to us. Jacob did not believe that he was going to die outside of the promised land. That was not a conception in his mind. He knew that he was going to see the promise of God fulfilled in his lifetime. When he laid down on the rock stone and the Lord showed him the Ladder of Divine Ascent, he realized, "What! Surely, the Lord is in this place! I can take Him at His Word, and I will see it happen in my lifetime!"

Jacob knew that he would not die without the freedom that was promised to him. That was not going to happen - even if he had to use Holy cunning. Yes. Holy cunning.

Even if he had to use Holy cunning, he was going to collect that which had been promised to him. Even if he had to wrestle with God, he was going to see the promise fulfilled in his lifetime. Brothers and sisters, this is the importance of an Abrahamic faith.

We always proclaim to have an Abrahamic faith. Of the three religions of the Abrahamic tradition, our claim to righteousness and holiness is Abraham, our father. It's like the Jews in the time of the Old Testament who said, "We have Abraham as our father!" Then Jesus told them that if He wanted, he could make stones the children of Abraham.

This is the importance of having an Abrahamic faith. We worship the God of Abraham, Isaac, and Jacob. Should we not worship Him the same way that they worshiped? Should we not commit to seeing the fulfillment of these promises of God to us and our people, *in our lifetime*?

Cease your doubt of God's power. Let go of your thoughts that characterize God as apathetic to our plight with the erroneous notion that somehow, He is absent or doesn't care. Don't buy into the idea that He isn't interested or is unwilling to fulfill the promises that He made to us in our lifetime. Cast down the viewpoint that He must be forgetful of the promises that He has made, that He is reneging, or is somehow a God Who would deceive us and promise one thing (like Laban) with no intention of giving what He promised.

We must cease to allow White power to thwart or delay the promises of God to us. We must not allow them to determine when and how God's promises to us ought to be fulfilled.

What does that mean? Really? It means that we are to reconnect with the righteousness of our request when the promise was made.

Think on the story of Jacob with all the twists and turns, deception, lies, and cheating. When you think deeply on the story, you might find yourself thinking "where's the holiness in this?!", and that would be a fair thought.

Jacob may have been deceitful in taking "Esau's" blessing from Isaac. Jacob may seem deceitful in how he procured the cattle from Laban, but we must also remember that Jacob made all those agreements with sincerity.

Jacob didn't just try to steal his brother's birthright. Jacob identified that his brother didn't care about his birthright and Jacob made a deal; it was an honest deal with his brother for the birthright. Jacob did what he was supposed to do to gain control of the birthright.

What's the problem?

Jacob told Laban straight out, "I will serve you for your younger daughter." That's what he said. After Jacob fulfilled his terms of the agreement, Laban *then* clarified that his customs rendered their honest deal invalid?! Laban and Jacob made an agreement for cattle, but when the deal didn't work out in Laban's favor, he switched the deal to reclaim advantage. Still, Jacob was not deterred. Rather, he relied on the righteousness of his request.

When our people requested freedom, there was no conniving. There was no deceit. There was no guile in our request. It was a righteous request. To understand the righteousness of our request for the mattering of our lives, we must identify the character of one who would make promises in such a situation and have, up to now, failed to fulfill. Let us identify the character of a people who can see the heinousness that they did, make promises to rectify the situation, and make recompense to right the wrongs committed against their American "brothers and sisters." Identify the character of a people who could make such a promise and find a "reason" why fulfillment is yet to come. Is there any reason why you should still be waiting and begging for them to fulfill the promises that they supposedly made?

Identify the character of one who has continuously made excuses for delay. Then, think about what would have to happen for you to respond like Jacob.

The Lord said to Jacob, "What is your name?" He said, "Jacob." The Lord said, "Your name shall no longer be Jacob, but Israel; for you have prevailed with God and with men."

Jacob was determined to get what had been promised to him by those who had promised. He got the birthright from his brother Esau. He got the daughter and the cattle from Laban. Then, he procured the promise from the Lord. He had honestly approached each promise that had been made to him. He did not make any request deceitfully.

What needs to happen for you to become like Jacob — to prevail against those who have promised and denied fulfillment of their promise — so that you can receive what has been promised? We must identify the character of God.

In Genesis 28:15, the Lord said to Jacob, "I will not leave you until I have done what I have spoken to you." In other places of the Word, the Lord reminds of His Divine Intentionality. We always talk about the importance of intentionality and what it means, and the Word consistently reminds us of the Lord's Divine Intentionality and His Faithfulness.

What needs to happen for you to hold Him accountable to His Word? That's what Jacob was doing. He said, "I'm going to wrestle with You because You owe me a blessing. You said You were going to bless me, and here I am still on the run with no place for my head. I've been trying my best to live faithfully. Yes, I have fallen, but I have gotten up. I have been faithful to your word. You made a promise to me, Lord, and I will not let you go until you bless me!"

Jacob was holding the Lord accountable to His Word. What would compel you to wrestle with the Lord? What would you need to understand about what He has allowed us to experience? As a Black man or woman, how has He left you, and how has He left us as Black people on the run like Jacob?

This does not negate the myriad blessings of life and the earthly blessings that you might be fortunate to enjoy. Again, Jacob was blessed; he had luxuries and material wealth. Jacob had two wives! Lord knows that one is enough, but Jacob had two wives and plenty of cattle. Blessed is the man whose quiver is full of children! Jacob had 12! Well, it was 11 at that time. Still, that's many mouths to feed, and he could feed them all just fine; they didn't want for food.

We have good lives and nice things. We have great experiences and all kinds of things at our disposal. We even have material wealth, but like Jacob, we are still on the run with no place to rest our head. There's no space where it is known that our Black lives matter, we don't have to fight to matter, or we don't have to teach our children about asserting themselves to matter in the same way.

What false piety do you have to overcome to even consider wrestling with God?

When I was in parish life, I used to tell people all the time to look at the psalms! David would rail against God. "Where are you? When will you come to me? Why don't you do something about my enemies?" Yet, we live our faith where you cannot rail against God.

How do you get what you need so that you might get what's been promised? How determined are you to get what you need so that you might get what has been promised? That is the question and the challenge for us. Are we committed to receiving the promises of God? Are we willing to do what we must do to see those promises fulfilled? Do we even believe that those promises will or must be fulfilled in our lifetime?

I worship the Lord, the God of our fathers, Abraham, Isaac, and Jacob. He is the One who made promises for the future, hence why we can embrace him. Thanks be to God. However, God made promises for the now because life is in the present. God is in the present. Only God is present. If only God is present, then His blessings must be for the now.

May the Lord give us strength and courage to remember His promises to everyone, yes — but to us. May He give you the courage to remember His promises to us!

It doesn't matter if you're from the Caribbean, it's the same deal. When we broke free from colonialism in the Caribbean, from colonialism on the continent, and slavery here in America, the Lord made promises to us.

May He give you the strength and the courage to dream of, articulate, and teach your children about the promises made to us! May He imbue you with that courage to see the fulfillment of His promises to us! Finally, may He give you wisdom that you might be cunning as a serpent and harmless as a dove in procuring the promise of God. In the Name of the Father, the Son, and the Holy Spirit — One God! Amen.

Chapter Four

Genesis 37, 39-45

Joseph's Dream

Now Jacob dwelt in the land where his father had sojourned, in the land of Canaan. This is the genealogy of Jacob. Joseph, being seventeen years old, was shepherding the sheep with his brothers. Now the lad was with the sons of Bilhah and the sons of Zilpah, his father's wives; and Joseph brought a bad report of them to his father. Now Israel loved Joseph more than all his sons, because he was the son of his old age. He also made him a tunic of many colors. But when his brothers saw that their father loved him more than all his brothers, they hated him and could not speak civilly to him.

Then Joseph had a dream, and reported it to his brothers. Thus he said to them, "Hear this dream I dreamed: There we were, binding sheaves in the field. Then behold, my sheaf arose and also stood upright; and indeed your sheaves stood all around and bowed down to my sheaf." So his brothers said to him, "Shall you indeed reign over us? Or shall you indeed have dominion over us?" So they hated him even more for his dreams and for his words.

Then he dreamed still another dream and told it to his brothers, and said, "Look, I have dreamed another dream. And this time, the sun, the moon, and the eleven stars bowed down to me." So he told it to his father and his brothers; and his father rebuked him and said to him, "What is this dream you have dreamed? Shall your mother and I and your brothers indeed come and bow down on the ground before you?" And his brothers envied him, but his father kept the matter in mind.

Joseph Is Sold into Egypt

Then his brothers went to feed their father's flock in Shechem. And Israel said to Joseph, "Are not your brothers shepherding the sheep in Shechem? Come, I will send you to them." So he said to him, "Here I am." Then Israel said to him, "Go and see if it is well with your brothers and well with the sheep, and bring back word to me." So he sent him out of the Valley of Hebron, and he went to Shechem.

Now a certain man found him, and there he was, wandering in the field. So the man asked him, saying, "What are you seeking?" He replied, "I am looking for my brothers. Tell me where they are feeding their sheep." The man said to him, "They have departed from here, for I heard them say, 'Let us go to Dothan.'" So Joseph went after his brothers and found them in Dothan. Now when they saw him afar off, even before he came near them, they conspired against him to kill him. Then they said to one another, "Look, this dreamer is coming. Come therefore, let us now kill him and cast him into some pit; and we shall say, 'Some wild beast has devoured him.' We shall see what will become of his dreams."

But Reuben heard it, and he delivered him out of their hands; and said, "Let us not kill him." Again, Reuben said to them, "Shed no blood, but cast him into this pit in the desert; and do not lay a hand on him"—that he might deliver him out of their hands, and bring him back to his father. So it came to pass, when Joseph came to his brothers, they stripped the tunic of many colors off him. Then they took him and cast him into a pit, which was empty; for there was no water in it.

They then sat down to eat a meal, and lifted their eyes and looked, and there was a company of Ishmaelite wayfarers coming from Gilead with their camels bearing spices, balm, and myrrh, on their way to carry them down to Egypt. So Judah said to his brothers, "What profit is there if we kill our brother and conceal his blood? Come and let us sell him to the Ishmaelites, but let not our hand be upon him; for he is our brother and our flesh"; and his brothers listened. Thus the Midianite traders passed by, and the brothers pulled Joseph up and lifted him out of the pit; and they sold him to the Ishmaelites for twenty pieces of gold. So they took Joseph to Egypt. Then Reuben returned to the pit, and when he saw Joseph was not in there, he tore his clothes. So he returned to his brothers and said, "The lad is not there; and I, where shall I go?"

Thus they took Joseph's tunic, killed a kid of the goats, and dipped the tunic in the blood. Then they sent the tunic of many colors, and had it brought to their father and said, "We found this. Do you know whether it is your son's tunic or not?" So he recognized it and said, "This is my son's tunic. A wild animal has devoured Joseph and carried him off." Then Jacob tore his clothes, put sackcloth on his waist, and mourned for his son many days. Thus all his sons and daughters arose to comfort him; but he refused to be comforted, and he said, "I shall go down into the grave to my son in mourning." So his father wept for him. Now the Midianites had sold him in Egypt to Potiphar, an officer of Pharaoh and captain of the guard.

Joseph Imprisoned in Egypt

Now Joseph had been taken down to Egypt, and Potiphar, Pharaoh's eunuch and captain of the guard, an Egyptian, had bought him from the Ishmaelites who had taken him down there. The Lord was with Joseph, and he was a successful man; and he was living in the house of his lord the Egyptian. So his lord saw that the Lord was with him and the Lord made all he did to prosper in his hand. Thus Joseph found grace in his sight and was pleasing to him. Then he made him overseer of his house, and put everything he had under Joseph's authority. So it was, from the time he made him overseer of his house and all he had, that the Lord blessed the Egyptian's house for Joseph's sake; and the blessing of the Lord was on all he had in the house and in the field. Thus he left all he had in Joseph's hand, and did not know what he had except for the bread he ate. Now Joseph was handsome in form and appearance.

Then it came to pass after these things that his lord's wife cast longing eyes on Joseph, and she said, "Lie with me." But he refused and said to his lord's wife, "Look, my lord does not know what is with me in the house and has committed all he has to my hand. There is no one greater in this house than I, nor has he kept back anything from me but you, because you are his wife. How then can I do this great wickedness, and sin against God?" So it was, as she spoke to Joseph day by day, that he did not heed her, to lie with her or to have relations with her. But it happened about this time, when Joseph went into the house to do his work, and none of the men of the house was inside, she caught him by his garment, saying, "Lie with me." But he left his garment in her hand, and fled and ran outside.

So it was, when she saw he had left his garment in her hand and fled outside, she called to the men of her house and spoke to them, saying, "See, he brought in to us a Hebrew to mock us. He came in to me to lie with me, and I cried out with a loud voice. Thus it happened, when he heard that I lifted my voice and cried out, he left his garment with me, and fled and went outside." So she kept his garment with her until his lord came home. Then she spoke to him with words like these, saying, "The Hebrew servant you brought to us came in to me to mock me; so it happened, as I lifted my voice and cried out, he left his garment with me and fled outside." So it was, when his lord heard the words his wife spoke to him, saying, "Your servant did to me after this manner," his anger was aroused. Then Joseph's lord took him and put him into the prison, a place where the king's prisoners were confined.

But the Lord was with Joseph and showed him mercy, and He gave him grace in the sight of the chief prison keeper. So the chief keeper of the prison put under Joseph's authority both the prison and all the prisoners, and whatever they did there. The chief keeper of the prison did not look into anything under Joseph's authority, because the Lord was with him; and whatever he did, the Lord made it prosper.

Joseph Interprets the Dreams of the Prisoners

Now it came to pass after these things, that the king of Egypt's chief cupbearer and chief baker offended their lord, the king of Egypt. So Pharaoh was angry with his two eunuchs, the chief cupbearer and the chief baker. Thus he put them in custody with the chief bodyguard in the prison, the place where Joseph was confined. Then the chief jailer committed them to Joseph, and he attended them; so they were in custody for a while.

Then the king of Egypt's chief cupbearer and the chief baker, who were confined in the prison, had a dream, both of them, each man's dream in one night and each man's dream with its own interpretation. So Joseph came in to them in the morning and looked at them, and saw they were troubled. Thus he asked Pharaoh's eunuchs, who were with him in the custody of his lord, saying, "Why do you look so sad today?" So they said to him, "We each had a dream, and there is no one to interpret it." Then Joseph said to them, "Do not interpretations belong to God? Therefore, relate them to me." Then the chief cupbearer related his dream to Joseph, and said to him, "Behold, in my dream a vine was before me, and in the vine were three branches; it was as though it budded, its blossoms shot forth, and its clusters brought forth ripe grapes. Then Pharaoh's cup was in my hand; and I took the grapes and pressed them into Pharaoh's cup, and placed the cup in Pharaoh's hand."

And Joseph said to him, "This is the interpretation of it: The three branches are three days. Now within three days Pharaoh will remember your position and restore your office of chief cupbearer; and you will put Pharaoh's cup in his hand according to the former manner, when you were his cupbearer. But remember me when it is well with you, and have mercy on me; make mention of me to Pharaoh, and get me out of this prison. For indeed I was stolen away from the land of the Hebrews; and I also have done nothing for them to put me into the dungeon."

When the chief baker saw the interpretation was good, he said to Joseph, "I also had a dream, and there were three white baskets on my head. In the uppermost basket were all kinds of baked goods for Pharaoh, and the birds ate them out of the basket on my head." So Joseph answered and said, "This is the interpretation of it: The three baskets are three days. Within three days Pharaoh will lift off your head from you and hang you on a tree; and the birds will eat your flesh from you."

Now it came to pass on the third day, which was Pharaoh's birthday, that he made a feast for all his servants; and he remembered the positions of his chief cupbearer and chief baker among his servants. Then he restored the chief cupbearer to his position, and he placed the cup in Pharaoh's hand. But he hanged the chief baker, as Joseph had interpreted to them. Yet the chief cupbearer did not remember Joseph, but forgot him.

Joseph Interprets the Dreams of Pharaoh

Then it came to pass, at the end of two full years, that Pharaoh had a dream; and behold, he stood by the river. Suddenly there came up out of the river seven cows, fine-looking and fat; and they fed in the meadow. Then behold, seven other cows came up after them out of the river, ugly and gaunt, and stood by the other cows on the bank of the river. But the ugly and gaunt cows ate up the seven fine-looking and fat cows. So Pharaoh awoke. He slept and dreamed a second time; and suddenly seven ears of corn came up on one stalk, plump and good. Then behold, seven ears of corn, thin and blighted by the east wind, sprang up after them. But the seven thin ears of corn devoured the seven plump and full ears. So Pharaoh awoke, and indeed, it was a dream.

Now it came to pass in the morning that his spirit was troubled, and he sent and called for all the interpreters of Egypt and all its wise men. Thus Pharaoh told them his dreams, but there was no one who could interpret them for Pharaoh. Then the cupbearer spoke to Pharaoh, saying, "I remember my sin this day. When Pharaoh was angry with his servants, and put me in custody in the house of the chief bodyguard, both myself and the chief baker, we each had a dream in one night, both he and I. Each had a dream regarding himself. Now there was with us a young Hebrew servant of the chief bodyguard, and we related our dreams to him; and he interpreted them for us. And it came to pass, just as he interpreted for us, so it happened. He restored me to my office, but he hanged him."

Then Pharaoh sent and called Joseph, and they brought him quickly out of the dungeon; and he shaved, changed his clothing, and came to Pharaoh. Thus Pharaoh said to Joseph, "I had a dream, and there is no one who can interpret it. But I heard it said of you that you can understand a dream, to interpret it." So Joseph answered Pharaoh, saying, "It is not in me; God will give Pharaoh an answer of peace."

Then Pharaoh said to Joseph, "Behold, in my dream I stood on the bank of the river. Suddenly seven cows came up out of the river, fine-looking and fat; and they fed in the meadow. Then behold, seven other cows came up after them, poor and very ugly and gaunt, such ugliness as I have never seen in all the land of Egypt. And the gaunt and ugly cows ate up the first seven, the fat cows. When they had eaten them, no one would have known they had eaten them, for they were just as ugly as at the beginning. So I awoke and fell asleep again. Again, I saw in my dream, and suddenly seven ears of corn came up on one stalk, full and good. Then behold, seven ears of corn, withered, thin, and blighted by the east wind, sprang up after them. But the thin ears of corn devoured the seven good ears. So I told all this to the interpreters, but there was no one who could explain it to me."

In the name of the Father, the Son, and the Holy Spirit — One God! Amen.

We give thanks to the Lord, our God, for his blessings in our lives, amen. He, indeed, is the one who gives us health and strength and who calls us into being, amen. He alone is the source of our mattering. Oh Lord, give us strength and courage to see you as the source of all things and to stand firm in your Word, believing and pursuing you in this day and ever more. Amen.

For a while now, we've been talking about becoming beloved community and embracing the promises of God for our people — Black people — as we are in this whole Black Lives Matter pandemic. As we continue to experience the direct and indirect effects of this pandemic, we must understand the basic level of commonality integrated throughout the many talks and meditations that we've had. It is this idea and desire for Black life to matter, right? That's what we want, right? We want Black lives to matter. We want to be able to say that we no longer must be out in the streets ever again because Black lives matter. We want an existence where the mattering of Black lives is a given and not just a given in word, but in thought, deed, sentiment, and in reality, right?

That's what we want. So, we're pursuing that. We've been analyzing how Black lives matter in different ways like a kaleidoscope reflects a different light to allow you to see things differently based on how you turn it. We're looking at the various perspectives of Black mattering through the story of the fathers, Abraham, Isaac, Jacob, and now Joseph. Previously, we were examining Jacob's experience and considering his commitment to the promises of God. Jacob's experience was filled with challenges and betrayals. Despite the realities of his existence and the machinations that he did to claim the things that were said to be for him — even up to wrestling with the Lord — we see that he was determined to see the promises fulfilled in his lifetime.

Yes, promises were made that he would have a family like dust in the wind beyond all expectations, but he still wanted to see its fulfillment in his lifetime. So, we started with Jacob, and we explored his willingness to even wrestle with God for reassurance of his blessing, demanding that God bring him to that place where he would no longer be on the run.

Yes, he prospered under Laban. He had the wives, livestock, children, and all sorts of blessedness. He had prospered, but he was still in a position of being on the run. He was still not certain about his existence. Not that any of us can be certain, but as he was going to meet his brother, Jacob still had to consider and divide his family, so that his entire family would not be conquered if Esau was still at rage with him. Jacob was still running from this place to that place. He was still on the run, and he demanded that God bring him to a place of peace where he would no longer be on the run.

We've recently been following the story of Joseph and how he was sold into slavery by his own brothers. We've been considering the similarity of his experience with ours as Blacks in America, in the Western hemisphere, and as the African descendants of slavery, be it in the Americas of North America, South America, and/or Caribbean America. We consider the experience of descendants from those who were sold into bondage by the ancestors of our brothers and sisters on the continent of Africa, connecting the mattering of Black life to our creation in our Blackness, in the imago Dei.

So, we've been looking at this issue of the mattering of Black lives or the issue of Black Lives Matter and trying to shift our focus in the foundation of that mattering, right? It's almost like the foundation of that mattering in public discourse is on the basis of White American or European society where all of these things have flared up. It is about a mattering in the foundations of White society. What we've been exploring is the ability to connect that mattering of Black life to our creation in our Blackness in the imago Dei. Our creation in the image of

God and our Blackness, is the source and the foundation of our mattering. Thanks be to God.

Today, we continue this quest for anamnesis — for that remembering which makes us present in the time that was given, right? I'm referring to the type of anamnesis that brings the past into the present, like Sankofa, which goes back to fetch the past so that we understand where we are going. Today, we continue this quest for anamnesis to remember the promises of God to our people and our ancestors who were freed from slavery. This is an important text for us who are the descendants of those who were sold into slavery by the African tribes that aided in the Slave Trade. We should pay close attention to this passage about the meeting with Joseph, the ruler over Egypt, as a man with power who was faced with the opportunity to get even with those who had sold him and left him for dead.

We will explore how his sense of self through the image of God conditioned his response towards his brothers and how he found the mattering of his life, despite the opinions and actions of others around him. We want to overcome the obstacles that keep us from embracing the redemption offered in Christ Jesus to us Black people.

If we think about it, we're doing all of this because we have no desire for spiritual connection to the source of our identity in the imago Dei. The source of our identity is the Lord God Almighty and the source of our *identity* in the imago Dei, specifically our creation as Black, is African. Our creation in holy Blackness is holy Africanness.

It's not like we were born then somehow dyed Black in the process coming down the fallopian tubes. We were created in the imago Dei. The expression of the imago Dei for us was and is specifically found in our essential Africanness. Again, we have no spiritual connection to or desire for reconnection to the source of our identity in the imago Dei. Now, this may all sound very esoteric...very "pie in the sky."

Why do we have no spiritual connection to (or desire for reconnection to) the source of our identity in imago Dei? That's what you are likely asking; it's the logical question to the previous statement.

Without a connection or a desire for reconnection to our essential Africanness, our Blackness, as the source of our creation in the image of God, and our Africanness remains inconsequential. Blackness remains of no consequence, no value, and no substance. Blackness is just coincidental. Our Africanness is just a coincidence. If it is consequential, the consequence is generally to our detriment as is played out in the experience of Black life in America.

It is a limitation and an obstacle that must be overcome. Consequently, we have to study twice as hard and be twice as good because our Blackness creates this space where we have to overcome something before we can even get on the playing field to start moving forward.

Because we have no connection to the source of our identity, there is no spiritual connection that links us to the promises of God, our Blackness, or our essential Africanness. Our Blackness remains inconsequential to securing our mattering.

Therefore, our Black identity is rooted in struggle and our experiences in both the west and post Africa. To "struggle for mattering" is part of our life; it is part of our existence. It is the quintessential component to being Black — to struggle against injustice. To be Black is to struggle against White supremacy. That is what it means to be subjugated, dominated, and controlled by White power and to resist or submit in that struggle.

In the deep recesses of our psychology as Black people, it is as if we think, "What will become of us if we no longer have to struggle against White supremacy? Will we cease to exist? Who will we be if we no longer have this fight?"

Because we have no spiritual connection to or desire for reconnection to the source of our identity in the imago Dei, hope is limited. Hope is confined. Hope is constrained to a desire for a White benevolence. All we can do is hope that White folks will one day get it right, start to love us, and realize that we are humans too. The only way we can have a life in America is if White power decides to abandon White supremacy, right? That's the only way. If White power gives up this White supremacy, then we will be okay. Unfortunately, we are forced to put our hope in the ultimate good of whiteness.

The ultimate good of whiteness reinforces the narrative of White supremacy in that White power will ultimately get it right, and we will be spared of their wrath. How can our lives matter? How can Black lives matter with such a perspective? How do we ever matter if Blackness is inconsequential, and a strong Black identity is not welcomed in society? The only way for a Black person to be welcomed is if they dumb down their identity and dim their light. How can we ever matter then?

As I read this passage on Joseph, I was struck by Joseph's mercy and his forgiveness. How was he able to do that? As I think on it and wrestle with it, I realized some things. I want to see how they resonate. When we talk about identity and mattering, Joseph's identity was inextricably linked to his homeland and the way as it was revealed to and through his ancestors. Let me say that again. Joseph's identity was inextricably linked. There was no way to separate who Joseph was from his homeland. There was no way to separate who Joseph was from the way, the truth, and the life. There was no way to sever him from his walk in faith, and from the way as it had been revealed to him and through his ancestors.

It is that link to his homeland. It is that link to the way as revealed throughout his ancestral lineage. It is that way that enabled him to remain faithful. It is that way that helped him to hold on to his self-image without believing the word of his oppressors about his identity or accepting the box in which they had hoped to confine him. He was not subject to the systems and structures that they had set up to oppress him, to make him remember his place, and to submit to their authority.

Joseph's identity allowed him to deny the word of his oppressors. He was inextricably linked to his father's land and the way that was revealed to his people through his ancestors. His disposition was a true desire for reconciliation with those who had wronged him. For the Lord wishes not the death of the sinner, but that he would repent and live.

So, how was Joseph able to be so gracious toward his brothers, especially when we consider the relationship that he had with them after being sold? At this point, years have passed. He was a child when they sold him into slavery. Now, he's a grown man ruling Egypt.

Think about the historical relationship of Joseph being sold and betrayed by his own brothers and the psychological trauma that this situation must have put him through. He must have been subjected to an identity crisis wondering, "Am I crazy? I see these visions that I believe are from you, Lord, but this is what's happening to me. Am I crazy? Maybe I am losing my mind."

How is it that Joseph was so gracious to his brothers who did that to him? In addition to his historical relationship with them, we can look at his current relationship in which they don't even know who he is yet. Let's consider chapter 45:1-15 where Joseph reveals himself to his brothers:

Now, Joseph could not restrain himself before all those who stood by him. And he cried out, 'Make everyone go out from me.' So no one stood with him while Joseph made himself known to his brothers, then he wept aloud, and the Egyptians and the house of Pharaoh heard it. Joseph then said to his brothers, 'I am Joseph, does my father still live?' But his brothers could not answer him, for they were stunned in his presence. But Joseph said to his brothers, 'Come near me.' So they came near.

Then he said, 'I am Joseph, your brother, whom you sold into Egypt. Now therefore, do not be grieved or angry with yourselves, because you sold me here, for God sent me before you to save life. For this is the second year of famine in the land, and five years still remain in which there will be neither plowing nor harvesting. For God sent me before you to preserve you as a remnant on the earth and to sustain you as a great remnant. So now, it was not you who sent me here, but God, and he made me a father to Pharaoh, and lord of all his house and ruler throughout all the land of Egypt.

Hurry then and go to my father and say to him, "Thus says your son, Joseph, 'God made me lord of all Egypt, come down to me, do not tarry. You shall dwell in the land of Goshen and you shall be near to me, you and your children, your children's children, your sheep and oxen, and all you have. There I will provide for you, lest you and your household, and all you have, come to poverty, for five years of famine still remain.'" And behold, your eyes and the eyes of my brother Benjamin. See it, it is my mouth that speaks to you, therefore you shall tell him my father of all my glory in Egypt, and of all you have seen and you shall have hurry and bring my father down here.' Then he fell on his brother Benjamin's neck and wept and Benjamin wept on his neck. Moreover, he kissed all his brothers and wept over them. And after this, his brothers talked with him.

This is the word of the Lord, brothers and sisters! Thanks be to God!

So, here it is, they are in Joseph's hands. When his brothers first came to Egypt, there was a famine that affected all the land, and people came from all over Egypt looking for sustenance, more food, and a better way of life. Egypt was the America of its day.

The famine finally came to where Joseph's brothers were, and they went to Egypt to look for food. Joseph was the ruler in Egypt, and he recognized his brothers, but his brothers didn't recognize him because he didn't look the same. He didn't look like the Joseph that they remembered. He was grown now, and he was dressed like an Egyptian. They didn't recognize him, but he recognized them. Although he helped them, he put them through all kinds of trials.

We must remember the power that Joseph had. The second time they came back to him, he sent them back again, but had stashed his special cup in Benjamin's bag. Then he sent his guard to chase down his brothers and to accuse them of stealing, which they had not stolen...this time. Yet, they had stolen when they took him and sold him into slavery. Then they said, "Here, search our stuff. If anyone is caught with your stuff, we will submit, and we will serve you."

Man, their things were searched, and they found the cup in Benjamin's bag; Benjamin was the youngest. So, Joseph's brothers first had to tell their father that Joseph was dead; now they'd have to tell him that Benjamin was dead too. They had to wrestle with the fact that they killed Joseph and then got Benjamin killed — both were Rachel's children. This is what was going on in their minds. They were terrified because both children from the wife Jacob wanted and loved the most had come to ruin because of them. How would they go home and tell their father that Benjamin had been killed too? Remember, they didn't yet know that the ruler was Joseph and they fell before him begging for mercy, crying, "Please, please, please. Don't take our brother, Benjamin, please."

Joseph decided to have mercy, but he didn't have to. Let's look at the power of Joseph and remind ourselves of his level of authority described in Genesis 41:39.

Then Pharaoh said to Joseph, 'Inasmuch as God has shown you all of this, there is no one as sensible and as intelligent as you. You, Joseph, shall be over my house and all my people shall be ruled according to your word, only in regard to the throne will I be greater than you.' So, Pharaoh said to Joseph, 'See, I have set you over all the land of Egypt.' Then, Pharaoh took the signet ring off his hand and put it on Joseph's hand; and he clothed him in garments of fine linen and put a gold chain around his neck. Then he had him ride in the second of his chariots and they cried out before him, 'Bow the knee.' So, he set him over all the land of Egypt. Pharaoh also said to Joseph, 'I am Pharaoh and without your consent, no man may lift his hand or foot in all the land of Egypt.'

Brothers and sisters, this is the power of Joseph. His brothers, who sold him into slavery, cowered before him in fear. They bowed down just as he had told them they would. What do you think he should have done? We know what he did. He spared them.

As you read the story and it comes to its climax, what do we tend to think that Joseph was going to do in that moment? If you were given Joseph's authority and you found yourself in the same position of encountering the brothers who had wronged you so greatly, what would you have done? Joseph didn't retaliate, and we must investigate why. How? How did he have the strength not to take revenge?

You see, Joseph had not stopped believing the Word. The Word spoke to him and gave him a vision of his true identity in the imago Dei for which God created him. The Word made Himself manifest to Joseph, and he never stopped believing the Word. He never stopped dreaming because he never stopped believing. Though his brothers mocked him saying, "Here comes the dreamer," he knew the Author and purpose of his vision which was to preserve life and not to take it away.

The visions of his brothers, Potiphar, and the Egyptians were created by the evil one who endeavors to take, end, destroy, devalue, and dehumanize life. That was their vision. If he had desired to take their life, he would have also embraced their vision.

Why did he continue to believe when everything showed him that his dreams were some bullshit and downright ridiculous? Everything showed him that his dreams were nonsense. He said to his brothers, "My sheaf was on top, and your sheaves were bowing down to me. Oh, even the stars, the moon, and the morning sun have bowed down to me; everything has bowed down to me." As he said this, they threw him in the pit and sold him into slavery. He later found himself left languishing in the bottom of the prison forgotten about and left to die. Every step along the way, his life got "worser and worser," as Fr. Nelson W. Pinder would say.

Every step of the way, things worsened for Joseph, but he never stopped dreaming. Why would he continue to dream? It seems like a waste of time, right? He fell into bondage, he was lied on, and he was thrown into prison. He was wrongly convicted and left to rot in jail in the prison industrial complex of the America of that time. Yet, he kept dreaming because he was confident that God's image of him was far greater than the image of his oppressors and naysayers.

The image that was created for him in the Kingdom was greater than the image that society had of him. He kept dreaming because the vision of his dreams was far more to be desired than his reality. Why should he stop dreaming when he could see the reality of his existence? He could look at Babylon, Egypt, and America and resolve, "This is my reality. If I stop dreaming, this is what I must accept. This is the existence I must give into and reconcile in my mind. I have to believe that this is enough for me, and it's satisfactory for my life. This is the condition that I must have and consider it to be okay, to be well with my soul." After coming to himself, he may have exclaimed, "No, man. This can't be the condition for me. I am going to hold on to the dreams that the Lord God Almighty has given to me!"

To be disregarded was worth it in exchange for holding on to his dreams and the vision of himself. Think about it. He refused to believe their vision. He could have believed it. He could have slept with Potiphar's wife. If he had slept with Potiphar's wife, he would have still been the head of Potiphar's guard, running Potiphar's house. All he had to do was sleep with Potiphar's wife. If you look at the oldest translations, we see that Potiphar was a eunuch. Why the heck does a eunuch need a wife? So, if a eunuch had a wife, we could also imagine it to be possible that it was standard practice for Potiphar's wife to be sleeping with the slaves and getting her fix from someplace. That could have been the culture.

Joseph said, "Potiphar gave me charge over everything in this house, except for you." We don't know whether or not Potiphar told him that. That could have been Joseph's own integrity, like, "Yo, he gave

74

me control over this, he ain't say you, so..." Still, all he had to do was sleep with her, and he would have been fine.

Many steps along the way, he could have told them something to be removed from prison, but he refused to believe their vision. He chose to languish and be disregarded to maintain the vision and image of himself that had been given to him by the Lord God almighty rather than give up the image that God had given him to find favor in Babylon, Egypt, or America.

He knew that the Author of his vision was greater than theirs, so he refused to stop believing. Since he did not stop believing, he did not stop dreaming. Beloved, when you stop believing, you stop dreaming, and the converse is also true. When you stop dreaming, you stop believing. Are you still dreaming?

Joseph abounded in grace towards his brothers because he believed the Word and the vision as they were revealed to him. His brothers merely participated in the Lord's divine plan. As he said in verse five of chapter 45, "Now therefore, do not be grieved or angry with yourselves because you sold me here, for God sent me here before you to save life." He wanted to be reconciled to his brothers and sisters, and he wanted to be in communion with them. The vision that the Lord had given him was never about being separated from his brothers or from his family. The vision was simply about the way things would be organized within that beloved community.

St. Chrysostom spoke of this passage and what Joseph may have said,

Do not be hard on yourselves. Don't think that you did these things to me out of your intent. It was not so much from your malice in my regard, as from God's wisdom and infallible love, that I should come here and now be in a favorable position to provide nourishment to you, and the whole country.

Though they knew what they were doing, Joseph did not hold his brothers responsible. Hear Christ from the cross who said, "Father forgive them, for they know not what they do." Joseph understood that they really did not know any better. Since they did not know better, they could not do better. Because he knew the level of their intellect, as it pertains to the way of life and the things of God, he forgave them. He understood that it was God's providence for them, and for all that had resulted in his being sent into Egypt.

St. Chrysostom continued on Joseph's sentiments,

That servitude procured for me this position. That sale brought me to this prominence. That distress proved the occasion of this honor for me. That envy produced this glory for me. Let us not simply hear this, but also emulate it. In the same way let us comfort those badly disposed to us, relieving them of responsibility for what has been done to us, and putting up with everything with great equanimity, like this remarkable man.

Like Joseph, our bondage as Black people and our sale into slavery put us in this position of prominence in the global fight for the mattering of Black life. Indeed, it is a global fight.

I was just talking to one of my friends from Colombia and learning about the rash of killings and White supremacist violence in Cali, where they're trying to take the Afro-Colombian ancestral lands. In this global fight for the mattering of Black life, we are the Blacks who are best positioned to affect the solution. Like Joseph, who was trained in the ways of his oppressor, but faithful to his ancestors who helped him to excel, we too have been trained in the ways of our oppressor.

Like Joseph, we are the ones who, when in our righteous minds, are best equipped to keep our people safe and free from the evil one who is always lurking and seeking the opportunity to coerce us back into bondage.

Similar to Joseph, we must understand that our identity is inextricably linked to the land of our people and the people who sold us into bondage. The source of our mattering and how Black lives matter is found in how we have been able to reconcile all that we have experienced as a people to that fundamental source. Remember that you are dust and to dust you shall return. Remember that you came from a source, and you will return to that source. You came from a particular dust, a particular earth, a particular land, and a particular clay that was molded into you. Remember that your identity is inextricably linked to the source of your identity.

How do you think we would be toward the descendants of the brothers and sisters who sold us into bondage? How do you think we would be toward our African brothers and sisters? Do you think we would receive them in love? How are we toward them now? How do we receive our African brothers and sisters now? Whether they immigrate here or not? More importantly, how do we receive them and seek out their well-being while they are on the continent of Africa? Are we even concerned? How do we live as if we are desiring reconciliation with our sisters and brothers and our fatherland and motherland?

In Genesis chapter 45, verses one through three, we read,

Now Joseph could not restrain himself before all those who stood by him. And he cried out, 'make everyone go out from me,' so no one stood with him while Joseph made himself known to his brothers.

Then he wept aloud, and the Egyptians and the house of Pharaoh heard it. Joseph said to his brothers, 'I am Joseph, does my father still live?'

Brothers and sisters, St. Ambrose says of this passage, "Joseph ordered all to withdraw, so that he could be recognized by his brothers. For even as Jesus said, he had not come except to the lost sheep that were the lost of the House of Israel."

In other words, the Egyptians would have benefitted from Joseph's service. Yes, he would've served Egypt well and made benefit for them, but Joseph's existence was for the lost sheep of the House of Israel. It was for his brothers who were lost and in Shechem who had turned their back on the way and had gone down into Dothan, the place of desolation. His brothers were indeed the lost House of Israel, and Joseph was sent ahead to preserve them. To preserve them, he had to make Egypt strong because Egypt was the America of that time and Egypt would be able to give them assistance. Egypt could be a place of refuge to them. He revealed himself explaining, "I am Joseph."

St. Ambrose continued, "I was made manifest to those who sought me not. I appeared to those who asked me not." This was as if to say Joseph's brothers were looking for help. There was famine in the land, and they knew that there was food in Egypt. They were looking for help, salvation, and a savior. They needed someone to give them sustenance. They weren't looking to God or their brother who was the one sent ahead to help.

Likewise, our African brothers and sisters come to the Egypt of this age looking for help, but they aren't looking for their brothers and sisters who they sold and were sent ahead to help.

Joseph asked, "Does my father still live? Are things well back home?" He was concerned, not just for those who came to the land where he happened to have power but equally concerned for his ancestral land and those who did not make that migrant's journey. He was concerned for all. He didn't disregard his homeland and his people who had sold him. He had not thrown them away, and he was not apathetic toward their struggle. He was not lukewarm in his concern for their well-being. Rather, he was actively engaged in cultivating a relationship where he could truly be a blessing to them.

He had a mind toward not repaying evil for evil. His desire was to repay their evil with his good so that he could at last be reconciled to the source of his identity. He wanted to see the fulfillment of the vision created for him by the Word. Joseph was able to show grace toward his brothers because he remembered his dreams.

What is our dream? What is the Black American dream of the people on this quest for identity and mattering? What is the vision given to us by the Word? Brothers and sisters, that vision is a source of our mattering and is what will make Black lives matter. For Black lives to matter, we must reconcile our Black identity to the source of our Blackness and the vision created for us by the Word who alone gives matter and establishes our mattering. Beloved, that will be inextricably linked to the source of our identity in the imago Dei that is created in Blackness and Africanness.

So, I invite you to reconsider and even re-envision the fullness of what it means to go back to Africa. Burning Spear said, "No one remember, old Marcus Garvey, no one remember, old Marcus Garvey." As Burning Spear continued, "They stoneth him to death." We killed his memory, and his memory is only held by a small few because Marcus Garvey wanted to see Black identity — Black humanity — in the imago Dei receive her redemption.

Black humanity must regain a sense of herself in the fullness of her Blackness, as being created in the image of God. For that to happen, Black humanity must return to Mother Africa which was chosen by the will of our Father in heaven to be the birthplace and establishment of our essential mattering. We must do more than physically go back to Africa, but also mentally and spiritually. As Garvey said and Marley popularized, "Emancipate yourselves from mental slavery, for none but ourselves can free our minds." Likewise, we must emancipate ourselves from spiritual slavery and reconnect to the image of God in which we were created.

To that end, I ask you, "What is the single most important question you have about the importance of constructing a spiritual foundation that is rooted in the essential Africanness of Black identity in the image of God? What needs to happen over the next month? Let's give ourselves a deadline, right? What needs to happen over the remainder of this month for you to begin intentionally and actively shaping a spiritual perspective with the Africanness of your identity as foundational to your mattering?

Brothers and sisters, the Lord made you Black for a reason. It's not over and above why He might've created somebody else white, brown, red, or yellow — since we use colors. The reason you were created Black and not White has merit, value, efficacy, and purpose. The reason was not just for ourselves but for the whole of humanity. You and I must have strength and courage.

May the Lord give us strength and courage that we indeed might see our self-image in the image of God as we were created! May He help us to understand the intentionality behind which and in which God has created each and every one of us that we might embrace and give thanks for that intentionality of His blessing! May God give us strength to hold firm to His vision for us and His promise to us, not the promises or the visions of the world! The Lord bless and keep you. The Lord make his face to shine upon you and lift up His countenance on you and give you peace. In the name of the Father, the Son, and the Holy Spirit — One God! Amen.

Chapter Five

Exodus 1:8-2:10

But there arose a new king over Egypt who knew not Joseph. Then he said to his nation, "Look, the race of the children of Israel is a great multitude and is stronger than we; come, let us outwit them, lest they multiply, and it happen in the event of war that they also join our enemies and fight against us and so escape out of the land." Therefore he set taskmasters over them to afflict them in their works; and they built for Pharaoh strong cities—Pithom and Raamses and On, which is Heliopolis. But the more they humbled them, the more they multiplied and grew; and the Egyptians greatly abhorred the children of Israel. So the Egyptians tyrannized the children of Israel by force. They made their lives bitter with hard labor—in mortar, in brick, and in all manner of service in the field. All their labor in which they made them serve was by violence.

Then the king of the Egyptians spoke to the Hebrew midwives, of whom the name of one was Shiphrah and the name of the other Puah; and he said, "When you do the duties of a midwife for the Hebrew women and see they are about to give birth, if it is a male, then you shall kill him; but if a female, let her live." But the midwives feared God and did not do as the king of Egypt commanded them, but saved the male children alive.

So the king of Egypt called for the midwives and said to them, "Why have you done this thing and saved the male children alive?" Thus the midwives said to

Pharaoh, *"Because the Hebrew women are not like the women of Egypt; for they are lively and give birth before the midwives come to them." Therefore God dealt well with the midwives, and the people multiplied and grew very mighty. So it was, because the midwives feared God, He provided households for them. So Pharaoh commanded all his people, saying, "Every male born to the Hebrews you shall cast into the river, but every female you shall save alive."*

The Birth of Moses

Now a man of the house of Levi went and took as wife a daughter of Levi. So the woman conceived and bore a son; and seeing he was a beautiful child, they hid him three months. But when she could no longer hide him, she took an ark of bulrushes, daubed it with asphalt, put the child in it, and laid it in the reeds by the river's bank. Now his sister was watching from a distance to learn what would be done with him.

Then the daughter of Pharaoh came down to bathe at the river, and her maidens walked along the riverside; and seeing the ark among the reeds, she sent a maid to get it. So when she opened the ark, she saw the child crying, and the daughter of Pharaoh had compassion on him and said, "This is one of the Hebrews' children." Then his sister said to Pharaoh's daughter, "Shall I go and call a nurse for you from the Hebrew women, that she may nurse the child for you?" So Pharaoh's daughter said to her, "Go." Then the maiden went and called the child's mother. Pharaoh's daughter then said to her, "Take this child and nurse him for me, and I will pay you." So the woman took the child and nursed him. Now when the boy was grown, she brought him to Pharaoh's daughter, and he became her son; and she called his name Moses, saying, "Because I drew him out of the water."

In the name of the Father, the Son, the Holy Spirit—One God! Amen.

Blessed God, we give thanks to You for Your love and guidance, by which You have caused us to live! That you indeed have given us life and an example for the way that we can travel this way unto You! Heavenly Father, we ask Your blessings, we ask Your guidance, and we ask Your protection as we journey along this way that we might find our exodus from oppression to the safe harbors and beloved community of Your love, oh Christ, our Strength and our Redeemer! Amen.

We've been on this journey. Joseph and his brothers have reunited. He finally revealed himself to his brothers and let them know, "I am Joseph. Is my father still well?", and they all wept.

Then Joseph brought his family to Egypt because they were living in famine in their land. They came to Egypt where he had food. At Pharaoh's permission, they had some of the best land. They received this premium land because Pharaoh was so grateful to Joseph for what he had done. Joseph made Egypt great again, and the society was grateful to him. In their gratefulness to him, they welcomed his brothers, his father, and their families.

Now as we start the book of Exodus, I need to reference some deuterocanonical texts which are texts that stand outside the canons of scripture as prescribed by the church, especially by the Western church. When we pick up in Exodus, we miss part of the history of Joseph. In seminary, I studied the history of Joseph in the Ethiopian canons, "Zenahu le-Yosef." It provides the backstory for what was going on with Joseph. It fills in some of the gaps that were left out in the scriptural reading. In Zenahu le-Yosef, Joseph spoke to his brothers before he died and told them that they were to leave Egypt before the sitting Pharaoh died.

He said to them, "Make this promise to me." We see in the scripture at the end of Genesis that he made them promise to take his bones out of Egypt and take them back to their land. He also said to them, "Make sure you leave this land before Pharaoh dies." You may question what I'm explaining, or you may not believe it because I said this information is from the Ethiopians. You may be thinking, "What do Ethiopians know about Christianity? Christianity is a White man's idea. If the facts don't come from White people, then I don't believe it."

If you don't believe or you're struggling with any of that, we can simply look at the ending of Genesis. Why would Joseph say those things to his brothers in this time? Why would Joseph tell his brothers that God would surely visit them, bring them up out of this land, and take them to the land sworn to their fathers?

Joseph remembered his land and his people so much that he was able to reconcile with his brothers and those who had oppressed him. He charged his family to remember their old land and return home. Just as Joseph never made Egypt his home, despite how well he was living in Egyptian society, he advised them not to become so comfortable in Egypt as to make Egypt their home. That makes sense, right?

The reason why Joseph was who he was is because he remembered his homeland. Wouldn't it make sense for him to also charge his brothers and his family to remember their homeland?

So, Joseph charged his brothers to remember their homeland, and he died. Now, we continue this journey in Exodus 1:8-2:10.

Brothers and sisters, we are trying to find that thing that will result in the mattering of Black lives, and therefore, we're investigating Exodus. This is why we've been following these stories. We want Black lives to matter, but what will it take? What will it take for Black lives to matter in this country and in this world?

Here, we resume our search for "mattering" by looking at Exodus, the way out — ex-odus. This is the story of how the Hebrew people found themselves in bondage in the first place and understanding their way out of that bondage. How did they identify the way out of bondage?

We need to understand the Exodus in the context of our experience, so let's look more closely at the passage before I get back to the major points.

There arose a king over Egypt who knew not Joseph...

The Egyptians didn't like the Hebrew people, but they were still worried about having the Hebrew people escape from the land. The Egyptians said:

Look, the race of the children of Israel is a great multitude and is stronger than we. Come, let us outwit them lest they multiply, and it happen, in the event of war, that they join our enemies and fight against us, and so escape out of our land.

Though they were not in bondage yet, the Egyptians did not like them, but they needed Hebrews to stay in their society. Why? It's the same reason the White Americans need the nigger around. You've got to have somebody to despise in society to compensate for your own wickedness.

They did not want the Israelites to escape because they needed a repository for all their wickedness. They needed someone to blame for the debauchery, degradation, and whatever wasn't going right in society. They could blame it on those people over there rather than be forced to look at themselves. So, they oppressed the Hebrews, tyrannized them by force, made their lives bitter, and violently made them serve all their labor. Sound familiar?

I want you to think about this because I've thought about it. Along came a king of Egypt who didn't know Joseph, and the result was that a mother had to put her child in a basket and send him adrift down the river to try and keep him safe.

We must understand that the best that this mother could do was to send her child up a river where he could be raised by Pharaoh or Pharaoh's daughter. Take note of how we read this stuff, and when we don't spend enough time in it, we fail to see the connectivity. Like the Lord said, "Be cunning as a serpent, yet harmless as doves."

This mother was cunning, like a good Black mother and Black women have always been in terms of finding ways to get by, taking the lemons of White supremacy and making lemonade for themselves, and finding a way to make something good for their families. This Hebrew mother, this Negro mother, did her best to find a way to make lemonade out of the lemons that were given to her. In verse 20, Pharaoh commanded all his people. Since the Hebrew people were in bondage, they belonged to Pharaoh too and were included in his edict. Just like we were owned by White power, they were owned by Egyptian power. Just like we were expected to aid in the return of "runaways," the Hebrew people were expected to aid in throwing every Hebrew male child into the river.

I could think about *12 Years a Slave* or all types of things. You can imagine both Hebrew and Egyptian people surprised at throwing a child into the river. Since the order wasn't to drown the children, imagine a caravan of children drifting down the river. The instructions were for every Hebrew male child to be cast into the river, but every female could live. When we hear that every female should be saved, this ultimately tells us that the boy children were drowned in the river.

I doubt that was true. We know for sure that wasn't always true because of the story of Moses. We see this, and we must also imagine that it was more than just Moses' mother hiding their male child. She wasn't the first mother to think about these things. These are the things that have been going on. We would have to imagine that mothers and fathers were gathered discussing, "How do we save our sons?"

Genocide was happening in Egypt. The Egyptians' plan was to discover the answer to, "How do we kill off the Hebrew people so that there are no longer any Hebrews, and all are just Egyptians? If we kill off all the men and let all the women live, we can take all the women for our wives. Over time, we will wipe out the Hebrew people...just like that."

The Hebrew people and their elders must have been thinking, "How do we keep our people alive now? Man, we were living this good life in Egypt. We're on this fat land with all of this produce. We've got all this wealth and prestige. Remember our ancestor, Joseph? We don't really know what he did, man. Remember our ancestor, Frederick Douglas? We don't really know what he did either, but whatever he did, he made these White people and these Egyptians love us and we've been living good. How do we keep ourselves alive now that we are oppressed so hard that we cannot stand?"

I imagine that Moses' mother was not the first mother to think about how she would keep her son alive. What about you? Do you think that Moses' mother was the first mother to think about these things?

Let's examine the text further so that we can unpack how we know that she was not the first. "Seeing that he was a beautiful child...", they hid him for three months. What mother sees their child and doesn't think that he's a beautiful child with a desire to keep him safe? When she could no longer hide him, she took an ark like Noah's Ark. It was an ark of bulrushes daubed with asphalt, and she put the child in it and laid it in the reeds by the river's bank.

There are some key elements here that we must see. When Moses' mother could no longer hide him, she took an ark and she daubed it with asphalt. It says bitumen and pitch, which is asphalt. Asphalt is a very sticky substance. Have you ever noticed how your feet still stick to a dry, newly paved road when you step on it?

She daubed the basket with asphalt which means that it was still in liquid form. She put the child in the basket and laid it in the reeds by the river's bank. She was cunning as a serpent yet harmless as a dove. "I'm going to obey the edict of Pharaoh", she said. Since Pharaoh said that the male child must be thrown in the river, I'm going to stage it and make it look like this child was in the river and somehow was caught adrift. The current must've moved the child over to the reeds, and this basket got stuck in the reeds."

This is why I imagined a bunch of baskets of little baby boys floating down the river, and surely, others must have got caught in the reeds. Maybe another child was previously caught in the reeds and another Egyptian woman picked up that child. So, the Hebrew maid servants possibly had an idea, "Aha! You know what could happen again? Some asphalt!"

This is all speculation, right? This is midrash time, but hopefully it is midrash that makes sense. It's likely that the Hebrew women saw this happen and thought, "Oh, here's a strategy to save our sons!"

I say this because the text says, "The daughter of Pharaoh came down to bathe at the river, and her maidens walked along the riverside, and seeing the ark among the reeds, she sent a maid to get it." His sister was watching from a distance to learn what would be done with him, and we later see that his sister was also one of Pharaoh's daughter's maidens. She is also the one who knew where Pharaoh's daughter was going to go bathe, as I'd imagine they each had a favorite bath location.

We can imagine that Moses's sister had some idea of the character of Pharoah's daughter since she was the maid servant's master. She probably thought, "My master is a good master. My master has compassion." Therefore, she understood that if her master finds a baby in the reeds, her master ain't going to just kill him and drown him in the water or push the basket out into the water to float further downstream. The maid servant has a good master, so she would have compassion on a crying baby.

Moses' sister watched from a distance to see what would happen to her brother and to make sure that no one else but her master found the child because someone else would probably kill him. I imagine that Moses' mother and sister planned how Moses would be saved. As it unfolded in the way they planned, the sister came out and said to Pharoah's daughter, "Shall I go call a nurse for you from the Hebrew women that she may nurse the child?" She may have added, "Though I wasn't aware that you would find a child (wink-wink), I will arbitrarily find a random Hebrew woman to come nurse this child."

Pharaoh's daughter said to her, "Yes, go." Then the maiden, Moses' sister, went and called the child's mother, and Pharaoh's daughter told the child's mother, "Take this child and nurse him for me, and I will pay you." This is an example of turning lemons into lemonade. Amid oppression and degradation, Moses' mother was able to not only keep her son alive, but she also received provisions for her households to do it. She was paid by her oppressor to keep her own child alive. Be cunning as a serpent, yet harmless as a dove, right?

When the boy was grown, she brought him to Pharaoh's daughter, and he became her son; she called his name Moses. She called his name. Pharaoh's daughter called his name Moses because she drew him out of water.

So, what do we learn from this? What do we see? Brothers and sisters, when we talk about along came a king who knew not Joseph, we should understand that the Hebrew people fell into bondage because they made a strange land their home and forgot their ancestral home.

Along came a king who knew not Joseph.

Remember, I told you that as Joseph lay dying, he told the Hebrew people, "Leave this land before this Pharoah dies." He'd already prophesied to his family when he said, "One day, all of you will bow to me, even my mother and father." They didn't believe him, and they sold him into slavery for it. As we see, it came to pass, and his family did bow to Joseph's awesome power in fear and trembling. The Hebrew people disregarded his second prophecy when they stayed beyond the time that Joseph prescribed.

They were living good, and they didn't want to leave their land. "Now we have milk and honey. We've got opportunity, good land, legacy, and history. As time passed through generations, we became more. Man, look at how good we're living! This ain't our land, but who cares about our land? If I remember correctly, based on the stories that our fathers told us, we left our land because there wasn't anything good in it. It's not our land, but we at least have an opportunity."

Because the Hebrews stayed in Egypt beyond the time prescribed by Joseph, the best that a mother could do was to raise her son and turn him over to her own oppressor to keep him safe. Does that sound right to you? Why is it the case that this was the best a mother could do for her son? Ultimately, that is how she was able to keep her child alive. Because Moses' mother was able to construct an ark to preserve the life of her son for the people of Israel, there is a Moses. The same way the ark preserved life for humanity through Noah, Moses was placed in an ark to preserve life.

Why was that the case? That was the case because the Hebrew children, the children of Israel, were able to live well in a strange land, so long as those in power remembered Joseph, their ancestor, and remembered Joseph's contribution to Egyptian life. So long as the Egyptian people remembered Joseph and remembered, "Man, when we were in a bind, man, this guy came along and look what he did. He brought us to prosperity. Look at the contributions. He built up our society. Look what happened, man. Because of Joseph, we can be in Egypt, the great society that everybody knows, loves, and comes to." As long as the Egyptian leadership remembered Joseph favorably, they lived well. The Hebrew people lived well in a strange land because the Egyptians, the people of the land, valued, appreciated, and remembered the contributions made by the first of the Hebrew people who came among them.

Along came a king who knew not Joseph. Along came a king who did not remember Joseph. It was a king who had no regard for Joseph and who did not give a damn about the contributions that Joseph had made. Then, society took delight. Society couldn't wait to start oppressing the Hebrew people. Oppressing them became sport. It was a distraction from the economic woes facing the Egyptian society.

This is similar to our present condition as Black people in American Society. Exodus 1:7-10 says:

The children of Israel increased and multiplied, became numerous and grew exceedingly mighty. And the land was filled with them. But then there arose a king over Egypt who knew not Joseph. And he said to his nation, 'Look, the race of the children of Israel is a great multitude and is stronger than we. Come. Let us outwit them lest they multiply, and it happen in the event of war that they also join our enemies and fight against us and so escape out of this land.

Understand, brothers and sisters. Understand. This was not new. The contempt for the Hebrew people could not have been new, but along came a king who knew not Joseph and had no regard for his contributions. He was able to tap into the vitriolic sentiment that existed amongst a section of the Egyptians toward the Hebrew people.

The children of Israel lived well in this strange land as long as those in power remembered what Joseph had done. However, when this king who did not have the same disposition came along, the latent vitriol that existed within the Egyptian people was ready to explode and come out in violence. And the hatred of the Egyptian people and their willingness to kill Hebrew boys with impunity drove Moses' mother to put her child in a basket. Does this sound familiar, Black people?

We've got to go deeper to better understand that the Hebrew people are not victims in this situation. Though the children of Israel lived well in the strange land, they erroneously made this land their home and no longer desired their homeland. They no longer had any desire to see the fulfillment of the promise of God given to Abraham, Isaac, and Jacob; the promise of God that nurtured Joseph and maintained his alliance and allegiance and kept him tied to his people and his land; and the promise that they would have a land of their own. The promise was not for them to dwell in somebody else's land, but that they would have a land of their own. Yet, they were living well in somebody else's land.

Because they were living well in somebody else's land, they said, "Man, who cares about that promise. I am not worried about the land that you promised to me. I already have this land right now. I'm not going to leave this land that I know and go to some strange land that you might give me. I'm not going to be like Abraham, Isaac, and Jacob. I'm not going to leave a familiar place that I've already known and become accustomed to go to a place that I do not know. I'm not going to take that leap of faith."

The children of Israel allowed the strange land to become their home. They no longer desired their ancestral lands or a land of their own. They did all this, despite the contempt of the Egyptians and Joseph's warning to, "Leave this land before this Pharaoh dies." Again, surely this new king was not the author of that contempt. Understand that just like King Trump is not the author of the contempt in America for Black life, surely this new king over Egypt was not the author of the contempt of the Egyptians towards the Hebrew people. This new king just used that contempt to empower himself and distract the Egyptians from the real problems that they faced. The Egyptian people, just like the White people of America, were more than willing to be distracted from the real problems and take out their frustrations on the people for whom they held contempt.

Brothers and sisters, here's the thing that we must realize and what I see from reading this text. The Hebrew people stayed in Egypt because they felt they had the good life in the midst of famine. They believed that Egypt was the land where they would always find a good life and they no longer desired any other land. They wanted a good life — not their own land and not their own place.

A good life can never be found in a land where your value is in question and up for debate. You cannot have a good life in a place where your identity in the imago Dei is up for question and is always out for assault. As we have seen with the rise of Trump, all it takes is for a king to come along who knows not Joseph, and every bit of security that you think you have found in this strange land is now in flux.

So, along came a king who knew not Joseph and had no regard for the contributions of Joseph nor the Hebrew people. We may say that it was Joseph who did good, but he was still part of the contribution of the Hebrew people. Although they sold him into slavery, they still deposited him into Egypt.

Israel's contribution was a result of Joseph being sent to Egypt. To have a king with no regard for the contributions of the Hebrew people was not the only problem. The real problem was that the Hebrew people had no value for the contributions that they had made and no value for the contributions of Joseph.

I'm sure it was good to shout Joseph's name. I'm sure the Hebrew people used to lift up Joseph's name just like we lift Dr. King, Frederick Douglass, Sojourner Truth, and Harriet Tubman, but they actually had no regard for the principles and the life that Joseph lived. Similarly, we lack regard for the principles and the life that Harriet Tubman and Nat Turner espoused.

Frederick Douglass said, "What to the American Negro is your 4th of July?" Still, every year at 4th of July, we're up in arms, celebrating "independence." We must honor our own contributions. Black lives will come to matter when we value the contributions that Black life has made.

They will matter when we honor them enough to sever our relationship with a people who can neither accept the mattering of Black life as basic principle, nor can they appreciate the value that Black life has contributed to whatever greatness exists in America.

We don't need them to honor our contributions; we need to honor our own contributions more. We need to respect ourselves enough to say, "No longer shall we be in relationship with a people who does not value us. We are not going to continue to be in relations." You would tell that to any man or woman if they were in a marriage where their husband or wife completely devalued them, they knew that their life didn't matter, they could do nothing right, and their contributions weren't worth shit.

Whenever you're in a relationship like that, good sense would tell you, "Man, you got to leave that sort of relationship."

You cannot be in relationship with somebody who you always have to fight to even exist. You know who you are and the value that you have. This little light of mine, I'm going to let it shine, let it shine, let it shine all the time. I'm not going to let you put it under a basket. The Lord said that I should not put it under a basket but on a lampstand, so I'm not going to allow you to put it under a basket for me! If you want to put it under a basket, I'm going to leave before you snuff out my light. Because I know my value, this little light of mine, I'm going to let it shine. I know the value that the Lord has placed on me, in the imago Dei, the image of God in which I was created. I know the value of my contributions to this life.

If people will give license to systems and structures that say I don't matter or have value, I will create a place where my mattering is never in question. We're going to become beloved community, with or without you.

This cannot be beloved. This can never be beloved if our identity is always up for scrutiny by those who, themselves, were created in the image of God. You cannot judge me; we were both created in the image of God, but Black lives will matter when Black lives matter to us.

What would it look like to honor our own contributions and give thanks for Black life? What would it look like for us to appreciate and be thankful for the Black life in which we were created without depending on the agreement of White power and the opinions of whiteness? What would that look like to you? How would you describe that space? How would you describe that ideation? What would that place look like for you?

Brothers and sisters, this is where we must come because there is surely a king who knows not Joseph and doesn't give a damn about Frederick Douglass. Obama, who didn't want to act like Joseph, ruled the land. Look how quickly a king came along that knew not Joseph. Anything that Joseph did, anything that Obama did, let's cut, cut, cut, cut, cut! Let's erase the memory, and the people were so ready to exercise their contempt for Blackness.

All they needed was a king to come along who knew not Joseph — somebody who wasn't going to appeal to political correctness and would allow the vitriol to surpass the boiling point. Father, forgive them, for they know not what they do. Let us not wait for them to get their minds right because their choice to reclaim their righteous mind is not a prerequisite for our restoration to the image of God in which we were created.

Rather than wait for them to give us permission to appreciate the imago Dei of Blackness, let's create a space where our mattering is not in question nor debated but where there is peace, love, and unity in the bond of the spirit.

So be strong and courageous to do what we must to survive in these times. Let us change the dynamic where the best that we can do is endeavor to turn our children over to our oppressor for safe-keeping, and condemn our children to do the same for their children and their children. This is a psychosis that must stop, and it can only be stopped by us through the grace of God given to us.

Beloved, let us walk worthy of the grace that is around us, within us, and that flows through us to value and show our appreciation for the image of God imprinted upon us. In the name of the Father, the Son, and the Holy Spirit — One God! Amen.

Chapter Six

Exodus 16:1-15

Manna and Quail

Now they journeyed from Elim, and all the congregation of the children of Israel came to the Wilderness of Sin, which is between Elim and Sinai, on the fifteenth day of the second month after they departed from the land of Egypt. Then the whole congregation of the children of Israel complained against Moses and Aaron. The children of Israel said to them, "Would we had died, smitten by the Lord in the land of Egypt, when we sat by the pots of meat and ate bread to the full. For you brought us out into this desert to kill this whole assembly with hunger." Then the Lord said to Moses, "Behold, I will rain bread out of heaven for you; and the people shall go out and gather a certain quota every day, that I may test them, whether they will walk in My law or not. So it shall be on the sixth day, they shall prepare what they bring in, and it shall be twice as much as they gather daily." Then Moses and Aaron said to all the congregation of the children of Israel, "At evening you shall know the Lord brought you out of the land of Egypt. In the morning you shall see the Lord's glory; for He hears your complaints against God. But what are we, that you complain against us?" Also Moses said, "The Lord's glory shall be seen when He gives you meat to eat in the evening, and in the morning bread to the full; for the Lord hears your complaints you make against Him. But what are we? Your complaints are not against us but against God." Then Moses spoke to Aaron, "Say to all the *congregation of the children of Israel, 'Come near before God, for He has heard your complaints.' " Now when Aaron spoke to the whole congregation of the children of Israel, they looked toward the desert, and behold, the Lord's glory appeared in the cloud. Then the Lord spoke to Moses, saying, "I have heard the complaints of the children of Israel. Speak to them, saying, 'At twilight you shall eat meat, and in the morning you shall be filled with bread. Then you shall know I am the Lord your God.' " So it was that quail came up at evening and covered the camp, and in the morning the dew lay all around the camp. But when the layer of dew lifted, there, on the surface of the desert, was a small round substance, white like coriander seed, like frost on the ground. So when the children of Israel saw it, they said to one another, "What is this?" For they did not know what it was. Thus Moses said to them, "This is the bread the Lord gives you to eat.*

In the name of the Father, the Son, and the Holy Spirit — One God! Amen.

Heavenly Father, we give thanks to you for your grace and your love! We thank you for the hope, salvation, and blessings that you show to us. Oh Lord, our God, we ask you to be with us and for Your Spirit to fill and transform us that we might transcend the limitations of our ideations and walk worthy of the calling to which we have been called. We desire to fully embrace the image of God in which we have been created, this day and always. Amen!

Blessed love.

I pray that all is well with you and that everything is on the "up and up" in your lives. I pray that you are feeling hopeful and that you have found hope in the midst of all that is going on. I don't wish for you to find a better way to *reconcile* yourselves to what is going on. That has been our way. We have become so used to hearing about another Black person being shot and killed that we are left numb. We've reconciled ourselves to what is happening, so that we might still have joy as ones who have blocked out reality.

I truly hope that you are really finding joy, blessedness, hope, and peace and that you are fully aware of all that is happening. It is especially in troubling times where the Lord makes His joy and peace known. Amen?!

We've been discussing about re-visioning of the imago Dei for Blackness.

What does that look like? What does it look like to be Black and redeemed fully in the image of God in which we were created? We've also discussed shifting our perspective from a Eurocentric paradigm to one that is not necessarily Afrocentric, but God-centric in which all of humanity is created in the image of God. We would see Blackness in the face of God, ourselves, and each other. So yes, it would become an Afrocentric paradigm, but also a God-centered paradigm because a Eurocentric paradigm is not based on God. Since a Eurocentric paradigm is not based on God, it would become both an Afrocentric and God-centered paradigm.

It's all about the mattering of Black lives. We want to come to that place where our right to exist is not in question. We want to live in a place where the people of the land would not even consider electing someone who believes us to be inferior.

We shouldn't be having a debate about which type of White supremacist we should choose. Black lives will matter when we can live in a place where — even if we didn't vote — there'd be no chance of anyone, regardless of race, color, or creed, to be considered for election when they hold such abhorrent views. We shouldn't be forced to choose between one who wishes to violently enforce our subjugation and another who simply believes that he can compel us to make peace with a certain degree of oppression, even if that degree of oppression is lighter than the oppression of the other guy.

The problem is that we prefer the luxury of oppression (Babylon) over the moderation of freedom. Therefore, we can't really consider or think about leaving the land of our oppression. The only solution is that this land will somehow become better for us. White power will become more amenable and compassionate towards us. That is always the only solution. We can't even consider leaving the land of our oppression because we are too in love with the luxuries and privileges of this life.

It's telling that chitterlings is a Black American delicacy. There are many other foods that are connected to our bondage, and we hold on to them as if they will make us feel closer to our ancestors since they ate these types of foods. We forget or ignore that our ancestors from prior generations ate healthy diets. The food of bondage is somehow made into something that is cherished by Black culture. While some are truly good, it's telling that we prefer the conveniences of White supremacist society.

We prefer those conveniences over freedom from White supremacy; we prefer access to White privilege. Other people of color who have straight hair and fairer skin can also put down Black people and be grafted into White privilege. However, we know that we can't be grafted into White privilege; we deeply understand that.

Nonetheless, we have access to White privilege because some of that White privilege falls off the table and the "dogs get the crumbs."

We get to enjoy some of the experiences, places, and things that white privilege affords us.

We have access to White privilege by our proximity to whiteness; whenever Whites move, we follow behind. We wanted to integrate so that we could be close to whiteness and have access to White privilege to have some of those things. That's why when freedom came, we didn't leave. We stayed despite having been whipped into submission the day before because of that proximity to whiteness and the access to White privilege.

We don't want to change our situation unless we can guarantee that we can maintain the living standards of our present situation. We want to ensure that our society resembles the supremacist society of our oppressors. Doesn't that sound ridiculous? Can you imagine the Israelites coming out of Egypt and into the wilderness?

We will now look at Exodus 16:1-15.

Brothers and sisters, verse three says:

The children of Israel said to them, "Would we had died, smitten by the Lord in the land of Egypt, when we sat by the pots of meat and ate bread to the full. For you brought us out into this desert to kill this whole assembly with hunger.

Let me say this in another translation. "If only the Lord had killed us back in Egypt," they moaned. "There, we sat around pots filled with meat and ate all the bread we wanted, but now you have brought us into this wilderness to starve us all to death."

You can't tell me that isn't funny! They would have preferred to die in oppression rather than live free. The children of Israel preferred the luxuries and succulence that came with their oppression — the side dish to their oppression. They were comfortable with their oppression because the privileges they had made their oppression tolerable. They were willing to accept their oppression if it came with pots of meat and bread to the full. They were incentivized by accoutrements and shiny luxuries to compartmentalize their oppression.

Like our numbness to the killing of unarmed Black men, the Israelites locked their oppression away. We see Black women killed in their home and all kinds of nonsense, but we compartmentalize and lock it away in the back of our minds. We are incentivized to do so by the privileges that come with this oppressive society.

We say, "It won't happen to me. That's why I went to college. That's why I got a good job. That's why I moved to a certain neighborhood. That's why I did this. That's why I did that because them niggers gonna get it but not me. I will be cool." So, we can't even consider freedom, what freedom is, or what freedom would look like — the gospel imperatives.

We can't consider freedom because we see the luxuries, opulence, and everything that we have access to on this side, compared to what we would not have access to on that side. I tell you all the time that I'm from the Virgin Islands. When we went up to the States for college, many of us had a motto which said, "We come up here to Babylon to get the money and run. We're going to get what we need, then go back home because we know this place ain't for us."

Over time, you get so accustomed to the luxuries and conveniences, like high-speed internet everywhere. You have city water, and you don't have to ration it. I remember when I went to college, and I no longer had to conserve water. In the Virgin Islands, we were born conservationists; you don't just let the water run! I was amazed when I came stateside, and I could just let the water run. I'd turn it on, let it heat up, walk back to my dorm room, talk on the phone, and come back when it was nice and steamy. Oh gosh, how luxurious!

In the Virgin Islands, you don't have high-speed internet everywhere in places like the hills. But stateside?! In these times, you must have high-speed internet. I find myself telling my mother, "If I come back home, I have to find a way to get high-speed internet because I can't live without it."

Nevertheless, this is the land of the free. However, in this place of "freedom" we have yet to find any freedom. This remains the land of our oppression. The 2020 Elections. The January 6th Insurrection. The 2022 Midterms.

How many of you think that there won't be another violent flare-up of White supremacy in this environment? How many of you really believe that there will be no flare-up of racialized violence? I don't know where it's going to be. I know it happened in Ocoee, Florida during the Ocoee massacre on a presidential election day 100 years ago. I know it happened 100 years ago in Tulsa, Oklahoma. I know it happened 102 years ago in East St. Louis. I don't know where it's going to happen, but you cannot tell me it's not going to happen...and you cannot tell yourself! If you really think on it, you hope it doesn't happen. Still, you cannot say. As you look at the times, you say to yourself, "It's getting real out here." However, just like the Israelites, we are so in love with the luxuries of our oppression that we can't even think about leaving.

I'm not saying that you must leave, but we can't even really give thought to leaving the land of our oppression. We say, "Yeah, I might be shot and killed, but at least I have high-speed internet. I might die with a knee on my neck, but at least Amazon delivers in two hours."

If we go to our homeland in a quest for freedom, we'll see meagerness, moderation, and lack. We'll see what we don't have compared to what we have here.

The Israelites saw that too. Man, that manna rained down from heaven then a tiny quail came up from the ground. The Israelites complained to Moses saying, "Man, it would've been better if the Lord had just killed us in Egypt where we had lots of food, bread to the full, and pots full of meat." And the Lord said, "I tell you what, I'm going to rain down bread from heaven and give you meat to the eat in the evening. Then, you'll know that I am the Lord." They responded, "Okay, yeah. That's what you say, so we'll see." Then, they saw this flaky, frosted sustenance come down from heaven.

So, tiny quail at night and a dust-like "bread" came up from the ground in the mornings. Have you ever eaten quail? Quail is small! When the Israelites saw the quail and the so-called bread in verse 15, they said, "What is this? What is this?" It seems like they must have been a little curious like, "Man...what is this?"

No, man, they were *vexed* exclaiming, "What is this?! We had bread to the full and pots of meat, but all you sent was quail? Lord, You sent this dust and little flakes and you proclaim Yourself to be the Lord? What...is...this?"

The scripture continues, "They say, 'What is this?' For they did not know what it was. So, Moses said to them, 'What is this? This is the bread the Lord gives you to eat.'" I think he was letting them know that which seems meager but comes from God is far better and superior to the opulent extravagance from your oppressor. This calls you to moderation because you don't have much; you only need to gather enough for today.

You cannot just sit lazily by pots of meat and eat bread to the full. You are called to moderation and diligence to gather only what you need in the evening and the morning. If you gather too much and become gluttonous, the food will rot. That which calls you to moderation is far superior to that which calls you to complacency and laziness.

You see, that's what the fat of Babylon calls you to. The riches and the privileges of Babylon and White power call you to laziness and complacency. They can label the Black man as lazy because we have answered the call of Babylon — the call to laziness and complacency. You don't want to change your life because if you do, you won't have the same kind of luxuries that you had in life.

However, the bread of the Lord should not be expected to be on the same level as the bread of the oppressor. When I say that the bread of the Lord should not be on the same level as the oppressor, a person of the oppressed mind may already think that the bread of the oppressor is up in heights. So, what does this mean? Of course, the bread of the Lord should be on the same level. Why would I step down to take the bread of the Lord?"

No, no, no, no, no. Renew your minds, brothers and sisters. The bread of the Lord should not be on the same level as the bread from your oppressors. The bread of your oppressors looks like it's abundant, but the bread of your oppressors is the truly lackluster and meager bread.

The bread of the Lord is far greater and superior. Don't bring the bread of the Lord down to the level of the bread of your oppressors. The bread of the Lord should not be expected to be on the same level as the bread of the oppressor. The lifestyle of Egypt was designed to keep the Israelites in bondage and to make them dependent upon their oppressor.

Yes, give them some benefits to convince the exceptional Hebrews to keep the many in line. Give benefits to the Hebrews' talented 10th to keep the 90th in line. Exceptional Negroes serve as an example of the benefits of docility, passivity, and to be bludgeoned over the head while claiming to turn the other cheek.

The lifestyle of Egypt was designed to keep them in bondage, but the bread of the Lord is the bread of the free. It is the bread that bred free people. Though clearly, freedom was not why the Hebrews wanted to come out of Egypt. They wanted power and lavish prosperity. They wanted payback and a chance to be powerful. They wanted this after all the power that they had just seen exhibited by the Lord?! They expected extravagance to rain down in a greater proportion than they had seen in Egypt.

They saw the bread of the Egyptians as being good for them. The bread of the Egyptians was the bread they desired. They licked their chops for generations hoping to get some of that Egyptian bread. They aspired to have the bread of the Egyptians. They were climbing up the social ladders trying to get closer to Egyptian power. "If God's power is greater than the Egyptian's power, then his bread must be way better than the bread we ate in Egypt. Man, I can't wait until He rains down this bread upon us! If we were destined to get just a little bit of this greatness from the Egyptians, imagine the greatness that we will get from God! Imagine the power that we will have!"

When the Lord rained down bread on them..."What is this?! Manna from heaven?!"

They expected extravagance to rain down in greater proportion than they had seen in Egypt. Like James and John, the sons of Zebedee, who wanted to sit at the right and left hand of His glory, the Israelites also expected to receive the benefits of the king. They wanted the opulence of their enemy. As they slaved in labor, the Israelites wanted all that they'd envied about the Egyptians. They saw the Egyptians' lives as a life of luxury, and they wanted the extravagance that had come to define power, success, and the good life. Having experienced the bad life, they wanted the good life, as defined by their oppressor.

They didn't get free to live poor. They were living poor in Egypt, and at least in Egypt they could play as if they had power. They could make it rain every now and again. They could go to the club and live it up. They could have spinning wheels and gold chains, and they could have dinners at the high-class restaurants and spas. At least in Egypt, they could pretend to live the good life. They were not satisfied with just the Word of the King, the Word of God. "This is it. This is all you've given me?" They thought that what was given to them was too meager, comparing it to the food that had kept them fat and docile.

The tiny flakes that came from the Lord were far greater than the lavish foods of their oppressors. The meat and bread of Egypt might have filled them for a night or a few days and made them feel good. I can see them eating that Egyptian food, drinking the wine, and probably singing the songs of joy in the midst of their misery and in their drunken stupor. They found a bit of reprieve that made them feel good until the next Hebrew boy was killed by the Egyptians; until the next Egyptian lorded it over them and beat the crap out of them for no reason; and until the next identity crisis that reminded them that they were not wanted in that society and that their lives did not matter to the Egyptians.

Between the killings, protests, and instances of not mattering, they could eat meat and bread until they were full, drink wine and be merry, and have a "good time." Still, the tiny flakes that came from the Lord were far greater than the lavish foods of their oppressors. Saint Ambrose reminds us of the food that God gives nourishes the souls of the wise. The Word of God delights and illuminates those who receive it. It's like the food that the Lord provided them was enough to sustain them, but not too much to make them docile and complacent. As Solomon said in one of the proverbs, "Don't give me too much that I may think I have no need for you or too little that I may despise you but give me just enough that I may ever rely upon you."

The food that the Lord had provided them was enough to sustain them. This helped them to depend upon the Lord and prevented them from depending upon those who would keep them in bondage. As Caesarius of Arles said:

If you desire to receive the Word of God, brothers and sisters, know that it is small and very fine, like the seed of the coriander, and understanding that we must come to prefer the food of freedom over the food of bondage.

There's a book I love called *Two Thousand Seasons* which is a story about captured Africans who overthrew the slave ships and returned to African shores to destroy slave castles and liberate other captured Africans. Now, you know why I read that.

Ghanaian novelist Ayi Kwei Armah has one character relay the problem that brought Africans under the spell of White supremacy, and this is what she said:

She spoke of those needing the White destroyer's shiny things to bring a feeling of worth into their lives, out of their deep-rooted inferiority of soul, and called them lacking in the essence of humanity, womanhood in a woman, manhood in men, for which deficiency they must crave things to eek out their beings, things to fill holes in their spirits.

However, the White man's shiny things will never bring you freedom. You know that, right?

The White man's shiny things have never been designed to bring you freedom. It is chasing after the White man's shiny things that got our people into bondage. It was the White man's shiny things that convinced kings, chiefs, and queens of Africa to sell other people into bondage and to turn other people into commodities for the sake of the White man's shiny things. The White man's shiny things will never bring us freedom, so how can we remain committed, compelled by, and drawn to the White man's shiny things?

We must desire freedom over all else. As they themselves said when they stole this country, "Give me liberty or give me death," we must desire freedom over all else. We must have freedom to serve the Lord. That's what Moses asked the Pharaoh every time he visited Pharaoh before a plague came. He said, "Hey, let us go so that we can go serve the Lord. Y'all don't have any regard for the Lord. We want to go and serve the Lord."

Desire freedom over all else. Desire the freedom to serve the Lord rather than simply begging the Lord for mercy from those who have complete disdain and disregard for the way of love and the Lord of love. Right now, all we want is the Lord to somehow convert people who don't want to be converted, when we know the Lord forces none to come to Him. We are begging Him to force them to come to Him so that we could catch a little break.

Rather, we must be more than willing to abandon the trappings of Babylon. It's funny that accoutrements and nice things are called trappings. You must listen to language. We must be more than willing to discard the White man's shiny things to embrace whatever might come in pursuit of that place where Black lives matter. What needs to happen in your life for you to desire freedom over all else?

You must confront yourself about your own preferences for the comforts of Babylon. We have them; I have them; you have them. You must confess them openly so that you can own them and be convicted by the reality of what you are clinging to at the expense of freedom. Then, you will be converted and will prefer even a piece of the freedom that God offers.

Right now, we want to hold on to a piece of the good that Babylon offers. We should be willing to do away with whatever good that is, even if it is only to receive a small bit of freedom in exchange for the freedom that God offers. That's repentance — turning from this way that has kept us fat and docile to the way that keeps us moving onward and upward toward the kingdom of God and the promised land. Let us march on until victory is won and let us not stop at the oases in this desert that trick us into thinking that we have found that place. Let us be clear in sight and of mind that by God's grace, we would make our way to the land of promise, in the Name of the Father, the Son, and the Holy Spirit — One God! Amen.

Chapter Seven

Exodus 17:1-7

Water from the Rock

Now all the congregation of the children of Israel departed from the Wilderness of Sin, according to their encampments and by the word of the Lord, and camped in Rephidim; but there was no water for the people to drink. Therefore the people contended with Moses, saying, "Give us water, that we may drink." Moses then said to them, "Why do you contend with me? Why do you tempt the Lord?" Thus the people thirsted there for water, and the people complained against Moses and said, "Why is it you brought us up out of Egypt to kill us, our children, and our cattle with thirst?" So Moses cried out to the Lord, saying, "What shall I do with this people? They are almost ready to stone me." Then the Lord said to Moses, "Go before this people and take with you some of the elders of Israel. Also take in your hand the rod with which you struck the river and go. Behold, I will stand before you there on the rock in Horeb; and you shall strike the rock, and water will come out of it so the people may drink." So Moses did so before the children of Israel. Thus he called the name of that place Temptation and Abuse, because of the abusive language of the children of Israel and because they tempted the Lord, saying, "Is the Lord among us or not?"

In the name of the Father, the Son, and the Holy Spirit — One God! Amen.

Father, we give thanks to you for the life that you have given us. Thank you for the witness of the ancestors by which we can know Your operation. Bless us, oh Lord, with strength, courage, and hope that we might see Your meaning for our lives and that we might walk worthy of the calling to which we have been called! Amen.

I give thanks to being in your presence again by God's grace. I hope all is well with you and yours on this trial called life that you are able to walk worthy.

It's not that you are always successful because we fall down, but we get up. It's that you are aware of when you fall or are falling and that you care that you are falling. Endeavor to maintain the unity of the Spirit and the bond of peace because all of life is about becoming. As long as we are continuously striving to become a beloved community, everything's going to be all right.

We're talking about building beloved community, and we've most recently been dealing with the mattering of Black lives. If you look out into the streets, read the papers, watch the news, or feel it in yourself, what we want is for Black lives to matter. The mattering of Black lives is all that we've been talking about.

And the Lord said in Matthew chapter five, verse six, "Blessed are those who hunger and thirst for righteousness, for they shall be filled." Today, we're going to talk about thirst because now, more than ever in my lifetime, we are thirsting for justice. In a quest for justice, we are willing to risk an encounter with Babylon, exposure to a pandemic, and voting for one White man in hopes that he'll be nicer than the current White man. Are you thirsty, brothers and sisters? If you are thirsting like our brothers and sisters in the streets, you want this thirst to be quenched. You don't want to be thirsting for forever and a day.

You want this thirst to be quenched. If we listen closely and endeavor to obey our thirst, we know that we're thirsting for justice. The cry and thirst are for essential mattering — thirsting to matter. We desire to live in a place where we never again have to humiliate ourselves to quench our thirst or confront men or women who need to see our humiliation live on the TV before they are compelled to grant us a little water to cool our thirst. We long for a place where we don't have to see mothers and fathers bawling and weeping on national TV, crying for justice or to see people so exasperated that they will burn down the only communities to which they have access — their own.

We want a place where we don't need for them to see people brought even lower than their comfort levels for them to take action and address our thirst for justice and mattering. That's what we want. Would you say that is the thirst for essential mattering?

The issue that we must contend with is that we really don't understand the depth of our souls' thirst for mattering. So, we continuously try to quench our thirst with things that only bring that thirst back with a vengeance. We quench our thirst in ways where every 50 years or so, we are faced with long, hot summers. We get so thirsty that we are willing to rage against the machine. This time, in this season, we're even willing to risk exposure to a pandemic that is disproportionately killing us.

We should know by now that despite whatever water they give us to drink, we will be dying of thirst again in another 50 years or so. We know that, and we're used to an environment where we must argue and contend with our benefactors. That is a way of life. That is just what we do. We march; we fight. That's just what it means to be Black. We do this. This is a way of life. To interact with a benefactor who only does good when contended with, tempted, cajoled, or provoked is a way of life.

Sometimes White power can be enticed by the allure of benefit. It may be for the good of their economy or whatever image that they want to portray in the world at this time. It could be good for this or that reason. Sometimes, White power must be provoked to do the right thing by the disruption of the status quo.

Therefore, we must sit in, march, boycott, or even riot before they are provoked to hopefully do the right thing. We have learned to satisfy ourselves with just enough water so that we don't die of thirst. We've conditioned and trained ourselves and our kids to be able to go long stretches without water, to endure thirst, and to live a little longer before we die from thirst. We've also learned how to tempt our American lords to procure enough water when we thirst severely enough so that we can endure Black life in America. This is the model that we are living out in America. We temporarily satisfy our thirst, knowing that we will be dying of thirst again later. This is the model that the Hebrews were living out in the wilderness, even after being freed from bondage.

This is what we see in Exodus 17:1-7, and I deeply want you all to see and thoroughly understand it. You need to see the Word. The Word is everything. The Hebrews were used to an environment where they fussed at and contended with their benefactors. Their benefactors only did good when the Hebrews contended with them. Back in Egypt, when they lived under the authority of the Egyptians, they became used to an environment after 400 years of oppression.

So, they are still tempting their Lord. That's what they're doing. They know like we know that when we want good from the people in power, we have to fight for it. We have to upset, exasperate, and contend with them. We have to march, protest, and fight. This is their new Lord, and they tempted their Lord as He needed to be enticed, allured, or provoked into doing the right thing like their Egyptian lords had needed to be. That was their way of life. That was the only way they knew that their thirst would be quenched.

Anytime they had a thirst to be quenched, they knew that the only way that power was going to quench the thirst was by contention, marching, and cries for justice. That was the only way they were going to receive any grace from these maleficent benefactors. So, they were still seeking to quench their thirst in a way that they knew would be cyclical and unending. They knew they would have to contend with their oppressors and lords again. They knew that they would have to tempt entice, allure, and provoke them again, but they also knew they had success from time to time in tempting their Egyptian lords. At times, they would be successful, and they would ultimately get their short term wants or needs addressed; their short-term thirsts were quenched. In this passage of Exodus, we see that the Israelites did not request water from the Lord as ones who knew and trusted their savior to provide for them.

Like their Egyptian lords, they figured that this Lord, the Lord God Almighty, would also abandon them. They thought their Lord would abandon them like those lords who would often give them a little water, turn off the spigot, then betray and dispose of them. In Exodus 17:7, it is written, "They tempted the Lord saying, 'Is the Lord among us or not?'" Is he still with us or has he abandoned us like all other lords have always abandoned us? Now we are out in the wilderness, and we have no food. We have no drink, and this Lord has probably already abandoned and betrayed us. He's already proved His point by killing the Egyptians. He may not be with us anymore.

Their way and all that they had experienced of their powerful lords in Egypt had conditioned them to believe that the Lord God Almighty would abandon them just as White power — I mean Egyptian power — had always abandoned them, but the Lord had just brought them out of Egypt. He had just parted the waters of the sea and fed them quail and manna from heaven.

Despite the goodness of the Lord, the people continuously griped and complained. They were about to receive their freedom while they still longed for oppression. They thirsted for the things of Egypt and their bondage. They did not thirst for righteousness or freedom. They thirsted for water when they should have thirsted for justice. They did not thirst for the Lord like the Lord thirsts for us.

In the Lord God Almighty's thirst for the Israelites' faith, He gave them water from a rock and showed them again that He was with them. I imagine He said, "Okay. Y'all still don't trust that I am with you. I will bring out water from this rock and show you that I am with you!" He again showed that He was not like the lords they knew in Egypt. This water from the rock was living water not standing. There are several classifications of water like flowing, moving, living, breathing, and standing water, right?

That's what the fathers teach. This is living water, not standing water. This is water flowing from the rock, not water that has been disconnected from the source. It has not been collected someplace to become standing, thereby standing and dead. This is living water directly connected to the source. God, the true source they were tempting, was showing them that He could make water flow from the rock, not just ooze. No, man. It's *flowing* water. We know living water never runs out. It never needs replenishing. This type of living water is ever present, and it is there to provide refreshment at even a hint of thirst.

We're going to dive into this because this is a complex idea. When we talk about this living water, we realize its importance, and we see it as water that quenches all thirst. We should want it, brothers and sisters. We should want it, Black people. We should want a way to ensure that we will never die of thirst again. We are dying of thirst. We are literally dying of thirst for righteousness, justice, and for mattering. We are literally dying of thirst.

Yes, we get Voting Rights Acts and renewals. There's this legislation and that legislation. We get things every so often to quench the thirst a little bit, but we are dying of thirst as Black people in America. We should want a way to ensure that we will never die of thirst again. I'll show you more about this living water. The Lord showed me and took me on His journey, man. We must look at John 4:5-30 which is the story about the Samaritan woman at the well.

John 4:5-30 says:

So He came to a city of Samaria which is called Sychar, near the plot of ground that Jacob gave to his son Joseph. Now Jacob's well was there. Jesus therefore, being wearied from His journey, sat thus by the well. It was about the sixth hour. A woman of Samaria came to draw water. Jesus said to her, "Give Me a drink." For His disciples had gone away into the city to buy food. Then the woman of Samaria said to Him, "How is it that You, being a Jew, ask a drink from me, a Samaritan woman? For Jews have no dealings with Samaritans." Jesus answered and said to her, "If you knew the gift of God, and who it is who says to you, 'Give Me a drink,' you would have asked Him, and He would have given you living water." The woman said to Him, "Sir, You have nothing to draw with, and the well is deep. Where then do You get that living water? Are You greater than our father Jacob, who gave us the well, and drank from it himself, as well as his sons and his livestock?" Jesus answered and said to her, "Whoever drinks of this water will thirst again, but whoever drinks of the water that I shall give him will never thirst. But the water that I shall give him will become in him a fountain of water springing up into everlasting life." The woman said to Him, "Sir, give me this water, that I may not thirst, nor come here to draw." Jesus said to her, "Go, call your husband, and come here." The woman answered and said, "I have no husband." Jesus said to her, "You have well said, 'I have no husband,' for you have had five husbands, and the one whom you now have is not your husband; in that you spoke truly." The woman said to Him, "Sir, I perceive that You are a prophet. Our fathers worshiped on this mountain, and you Jews say that in Jerusalem is the place where one ought to worship." Jesus said to her, "Woman, believe Me, the hour is coming when you will neither on this mountain, nor in Jerusalem, worship the Father. You worship what you do not know; we know what we worship, for salvation is of the Jews. But the hour is coming, and now is, when the true worshipers will worship the Father in spirit and truth; for the Father is seeking such to worship Him. God is Spirit, and those who worship Him must worship in spirit and truth." The woman said to Him, "I know that Messiah is coming (who is called Christ). When He comes, He will tell us all things." Jesus said to her, "I who speak to you am He." And at this point His disciples came, and they marveled that He talked with a woman; yet no one said, "What do You seek?" or, "Why are You talking with her?" The woman then left her waterpot, went her way into the city, and said to the men, "Come, see a Man who told me all things that I ever did. Could this be the Christ?" Then they went out of the city and came to Him.

"He came to a city of Samaria, which is called Sychar near the plot of ground that Jacob gave to his son Joseph." Now, I was thinking on this and the concept of thirst. When the Lord drew me to "thirst" in Exodus, I thought, "Where else have we found thirst and how thirst was dealt with when people were thirsty?" Of course, what pops into mind is when the Lord said on the cross, "I thirst." I see that too, but the woman at the well seemed like a more appropriate connection to thirsting people and how they respond to it.

Let me go back in the Word. The first line said, "Near the plot of ground that Jacob gave his son Joseph." I said, "Yes, Lord, your servant is listening." You all know by now how much I look at Joseph as a type for the identity and experience of Blackness. Like Joseph, we were sold into slavery by our brothers and sisters, served at the bottom of this land, and believed that we were the ones with the power to tap into the spiritual realm to make this country be what it could be. This would free the world from bondage to White supremacy. When it said "Joseph," I was compelled to pay closer attention. I knew this would yield some benefit for us.

Brothers and sisters, focus on this living water, what that living water does, and how it quenches the thirst. Drinking this living water is the way we should want our present thirst to be quenched.

One of the holy fathers, Romanos Malodus, said, "It was a season of burning heat. It was the sixth hour, as the scripture says. It was the middle of the day when the Messiah came to illumine those in darkness." When he came into that city in Samaria, went to the well, and met that woman, it was in the season of burning heat and the middle of the day — the hottest of the hot. If we understand the time right, it was customary for women to draw water in early morning or in early evening due to the heat. This woman came alone at noon, in the full heat of the

123

sun in this season of burning heat. This made an already arduous task of drawing water even more difficult.

Why would she do that? She did it because she was an outcast. The Samaritans were already outcasts, so she was an outcast of outcasts. Even among second class citizens, her society had created a world where she had to self-isolate to hold on to a little bit of belonging and connection. She wasn't kicked out of the city all together to live alone in the elements. She was able to stay on the fringes of society if she agreed to subjugate herself to the ways of their system and structure. If she agreed to humiliate and confine herself to the reality that was prescribed for her by the powerful men of that city, she could exist in a society of which she was supposedly a part.

She was supposedly a citizen of their society, but they forced her to conduct herself in ways that were humiliating, defacing of her identity because she had five husbands and was now a concubine for another man. That give them the right to deface her identity.

There she was at the well. When she approached the well, the Man was sitting there. This Man was the Son of Man, the Son of God — Jesus Christ — but she didn't know that yet. Nonetheless, when she saw this Man at the well, she was going to draw water. "Another man, sitting here waiting to see what he can get from me...," I imagine her thinking.

Everyone knew she drew her water in the middle of the day. That's the society that they ordained for her. They knew the hour they assigned for her. They knew how their culture and way of life had established the hour when she could draw water. They knew they didn't like the heat of the day, so the middle of the day was too hot for them to be bothered with her.

When she drew water in the middle of the day, she was alone —
no one else was at the well. She was vulnerable and there was a Man
sitting at the well waiting for her. Certainly, men must have made her all
kinds of promises. You know how men operate around vulnerable
women. You know how we do in society. They identified her "type."

"She's a prostitute. She's a woman of the night. I can have my
way with her."

Certainly, she's heard her share of indecent proposals from men
who knew all she ever did and wanted to use that to have their way with
her. They wanted to keep her in a vulnerable and precarious
circumstance and confine her to a prison so that she would remain an
object of abuse. They legislated her prison and set up her social structure
and laws that she obeyed. They established the "rule of law" to create
the social mores of her confinement and the limits of her interaction
with the world, even if she appeared to be free. This was the life she
lived.

The reality of living water was important, but it was not what
compelled her. Saint Theodore of Mopuestia said, "The woman did not
yet understand these words and did not know what living water was."
She didn't worry about living water. It kept her talking. She was
interested. He had game. It was interesting. It kept her engaged and kept
her talking. She wasn't like, "Oh God, here's another one of these men
with these ridiculous statements. I just want to get my water and go."
No, no, no. She kept talking. It kept her talking and it kept her open to
conversation, but it didn't make her move. It didn't sway her.

The reality of this living water is important, but it is not what
moves the people. Water is water, no matter how artisanal it is. If you're

dying of thirst, you won't care what brand name is on the label. No matter how special this water was, the woman knew.

She may have lamented, "No matter how special this water is, I will still have to humiliate myself to receive it." That's the way water works. As a matter of fact, based on the way I know men to interact with people, the way I know White power, the way I know Egyptian power, the way I know the powerful men of the city to interact with people, the better the water is, the more I'm going have to humiliate myself to get it.

"Right now, this is my humiliation, and I have access to the best well in the world. St. Chrysostom said:

It is as if she said, 'You cannot say that Jacob gave us this spring and then used another for himself. For he and his descendants drank from it, which they would not have done if they had another well that was better. Therefore, you cannot then give me water from this spring. And you do not have a better spring, unless you confess that you are greater than Jacob.' That's why she asked, 'Are you greater than Jacob? If you are not greater than Jacob, this is the best well that you could ever have. You cannot have a well that's better than Jacob's well, so where then does this water come from that you promise to give me, this living water?'

In other words, it's as we Black Americans would say, "the well of justice that comes from America is the well for which all others thirst! This is the well from which all others in the world come to drink. Everyone is trying to drink from this American well." We believe this is the best well around.

Although we come here regularly in thirst, we still know it to be the best well. You are not trying to live under anyone else's system. This is the best well you can envision.

The Lord let her know, "The simple reality, honey, is that as good as the water may be from Jacob, this may be the best well. As good as this water may be, whoever drinks it will thirst again."

Jesus "got game!"

You see, Jesus connected with her true thirst when he said, "Whoever drinks of the water that I shall give him, will never thirst. But the water I shall give him will become in him a fountain of water springing up into everlasting life."

On this passage, St. Theodore said, "Jesus knows of water that not only satisfies thirst, but that is also a source of perpetual refreshment." So, she would be perpetually refreshed instead of dying from thirst. Rather than daily coming to the well to get water so she didn't die of thirst, she would be perpetually refreshed. She would never thirst again. St. Augustine says that Jesus was inviting her to stop working so hard and to instead receive refreshment from Him.

She continuously humiliated herself to quench her thirst. Like James Baldwin said, "To be Black and semi-conscious in America is to be in a constant state of rage." It is hard work to endure humiliation. It takes a lot to code switch and to wear the mask of double consciousness.

I was listening to the Bank of America CEO Brian Moynihan, and I give credit to him for the things that he's doing. By God's grace, he'll bring them to fulfillment.

He says that his Black employees speak of the desire not to leave part of themselves outside when they come to work and pick it back up when they leave. May the Lord bless him for realizing that and give him strength to be able to create an environment where that doesn't exist!

Many of you who work for White people feel that feeling, right? There's certain sectors and aspects of yourself that you can never reveal in White spaces. It is hard work to know when to put down parts of yourself, to know when it's safe to pick it back up, and to commit to picking it back up.

It's hard work to commit to avoid abandoning and picking back up the pieces of yourself that you have left outside Massa's house. You might think, 'It's just easier if I kill off this part of myself. I don't have to keep going around the back of the building to pick it up and take it back home with me. Let me just kill this piece of myself and let it go." Hip hop is dead.

It's hard work not to kill off yourself and to endure humiliation day in and day out simply to quench your thirst.

This woman had to work hard. Jesus was inviting her to stop working so hard and instead receive refreshment from Him. "But whoever drinks of the water that I shall give him will never thirst." She would never thirst again. In verse 15, the woman said to him, "Sir, give me this water that I may not thirst nor come here to draw."

That's all she needed to know. All she needed to hear was that she would never thirst again. "Say no more, give me that water!" She had not been really persuaded by His other points when He said, "If you knew the gift of God and Who it is that says to you, 'give me a drink', I would have given you living water." That point didn't really matter to her that much, but the idea of never thirsting again did.

At this point, she was willing to abandon all that she had come to believe and all that she held sacred. She could release the various social structures that she obeyed. She was willing to instantly abandon all of that. The mores of society around her no longer held any weight. Their allure had been lost. They could no longer tempt her. She had no need to care if those with power made it difficult for her to get water because she would never thirst again! She had found what would truly quench her thirst once and for all.

That is what convicted her. That is what converted her. This made her willing and eager to embrace Christ and the way of love. She finally understood the real problem of her thirst. She wished to no longer be forced to humiliate herself to quench her thirst. She was motivated to never thirst again because she knew that she would never be humiliated again. She would be free at last. Free at last, thank God almighty, she would be free at last.

Brothers and sisters, I'm saying that we need to seek a solution that puts an end to our perpetual humiliation in effort to quench our thirst for mattering. We need to reject this way of contention for justice that has been prescribed for us by White power which only temporarily satisfies our thirst. We're marching and protesting for change knowing that we will be dying of thirst again in a few knowing that justice will ultimately not be just. I mean, come on, we knew no one was going to be indicted for Breonna Taylor's murder. We knew that. You can't tell me that you really thought someone was going to be indicted.

We know that justice won't ultimately be just. We know that the supremacist hatred is still present, even if electing Joe Biden makes it go dormant for a while. We know that we will soon start dying of thirst again and appealing for another dose of justice that won't be just. It's like the Hebrews who always wanted to return to Egypt and stay close to those Egyptian lords who were the same lords who needed to be enticed and provoked to do the right thing. They always wanted to go back. "We could have been in Egypt." In Egypt, all they could do was hope that along would come a king who remembered Joseph and would show some kindness to them.

They wanted to stay close to people against whom they always had to protest and argue just for even a small smidge of justice. They wanted to return to the land where their oppressors were in control. We talk about Maslow's self-actualization in the hierarchy of needs and the need in humanity, especially in the world that we've constructed in Western civilization. The Hebrews wanted to go to Egypt, but they would never be able to become self-actualized there. They would never see themselves fully and truly in the imago Dei. You cannot see yourself as truly created in the image of God if there's another human being that you accept as being Lord over you as an intermediary between you and the God in whose image you are created.

They wanted to return to the land where their oppressors were in control. In Egypt, they wouldn't ever be self-actualized. Though they may hope for the same rights and privileges, they would always see themselves as inferior to the Egyptians. They would not be entitled to the same rights and privileges. "Man, I wish I could do like the White folks — I mean the Egyptians." Occasionally they might experience a taste of the rights and privileges of whiteness — I mean of Egyptian-ness, but they would always see themselves as inferior to the Egyptians. While they would not be entitled to the same rights and privileges, they would have their basic needs met. They would eat. They would sit by the pots and eat bread to the full. They would have more than enough water for them, their children, and their livestock.

You see, their lives had no meaning in Egypt. There was no meaning beyond a sub-human meaning that had been established for them by the Egyptians. The Egyptians defined them and determined their meaning. It was only at the level of mattering that the Egyptians determined if the Hebrews would find any sort of meaning.

Lacking meaning and value, there was nothing even worth actualizing, so they longed for that learned security that they had found in Egypt. They knew when they would eat. They knew when they would drink. They couldn't count on much more. They would never know the full potential of all that was amazing within them in the imago Dei. They would never know a sense of their space and their place in this thing called life. They would never feel the joy of being a creator and tending to creation as defined by their own ideations of praise and thanksgiving to the God Who had delivered them. They wouldn't know that, but they could count on those basic needs. Those basic needs could literally be taken for granted. They wanted to be able to take that something for granted.

We are struggling to hope in all other areas of life; let us just be able to take something for granted. They were literally on the road to freedom with the ability to be self-actualized. Their greatest fear was loss of those basic needs. They could not see the greater need or see themselves as greater than what they had become in Egypt.

As it were, they did not see the need to dispel, discredit, or destroy the ideation, ideology, or image of Black inferiority. Let us not be like the Hebrews, who thirsted for benefits from lesser lords while they were with the Lord God Almighty. Rather, let us be like the Samaritan woman at the well who was absolutely through with being oppressed. She was eager to receive freedom from thirst so that she could receive freedom from subjugation. She could be free to see herself as greater than the image that power had designed for her.

Like that woman, let us desire to see ourselves as greater than how White power has defined us. Let us desire freedom from this perpetual thirst for justice. Let us seek the living water which alone can quench our thirst.

What needs to happen to assure you that some form of self-determination must be the solution? What needs to happen to assure you that no matter what, this is the case? We cannot continue to see being ruled by the Egyptians or White power as having any part of the solution.

May the Spirit be in our midst, opening our eyes that we may see what it is that he is revealing unto us so that we might find and become beloved community! Amen.

Chapter Eight

Exodus 32

Now when the people saw that Moses delayed coming down from the mountain, the people gathered against Aaron and said to him, "Rise up and make us gods that shall go before us. As for Moses, the man who brought us up from the land of Egypt, we do not know what has become of him." Aaron then said to them, "Remove the golden earrings in the ears of your wives and daughters and bring them to me." So all the people removed the golden earrings in their ears and brought them to Aaron. He received them from their hands; and he fashioned them with an engraving tool and made a molten calf. Then he said, "These are your gods, O Israel, that brought you out of the land of Egypt." So when Aaron saw it, he built an altar before it. Aaron then made a proclamation and said, "Tomorrow is a feast to the Lord." Thus he rose early the next day and offered whole burnt offerings and peace offerings; and the people sat down to eat and drink, and rose up to play. But the Lord said to Moses, "Go quickly! Get down from here! For your people whom you brought out of the land of Egypt are transgressing the law. They turned aside quickly from the way I commanded them. They made themselves a calf and are worshiping and sacrificing to it, and are saying, 'These are your gods, O Israel, that brought you out of the land of Egypt.' Now therefore, let Me be, that I may burn in wrath against them and consume them. Then I will make of you a great nation." But Moses prayed before the Lord God and said, "Why, O Lord, does Your wrath burn hot against

Your people whom You brought out of the land of Egypt with great power and a mighty hand? Why should the Egyptians speak and say, 'He brought them out with evil intent, to kill them in the mountains and to consume them from the face of the earth'? Turn from Your fierce wrath and be merciful to the wickedness of Your people. Remember Abraham, Isaac, and Jacob, Your servants, to whom You swore by Yourself and said to them, 'I will greatly multiply your seed as the stars of heaven for multitude; and all this land I spoke about to give their seed, they shall inherit unto the ages.' " So the Lord granted mercy for the harm He said He would do to His people.

Then Moses turned and went down from the mountain with the two tablets of the testimony in his hands. They were stone tablets written on both sides, on one side and on the other. Now the tablets were the work of God, and the writing was the writing of God engraved on the tablets. When Joshua therefore heard the noise of the people as they shouted, he said to Moses, "There is a noise of war in the camp." But Moses said, "It is not the noise of those that begin the battle, nor of those that begin the cry of defeat, but the noise of those that begin the banquet of wine that I hear." So it was, as soon as he came near the camp, he saw the calf and the dancing. Thus Moses became very angry; and he cast the two tablets out of his hands and broke them at the foot of the mountain. Then he took the calf they had made, burned it in the fire, and ground it to powder; and he scattered it on the water and made the children of Israel drink it. Moses then spoke to Aaron, "What did this people do to you that you brought so great a sin upon them?" Aaron replied, "Do not be angry, my lord. You know how impulsive this people is. For they said to me, 'Make us gods that shall go before us; as for this man Moses, who brought us out of the land of Egypt, we do not know what has become of him.' So I said to them, 'Whoever has any gold, let him remove it.' Thus they gave it to me, and I cast it into the fire, and this calf came out." Now when Moses saw the people were scattered (for Aaron scattered them, making them a prey to their enemies), Moses then stood in the entrance of the camp and said, "Whoever is on the Lord's side, come to me." So all the sons of Levi gathered themselves together to him. He said to them, "Thus says the Lord God of Israel: 'Let every man put his sword on his side and go in and out from entrance to entrance throughout the camp, and let every man kill his brother, every man his companion, and every man his neighbor.' " So the sons of Levi did as Moses said to them, and about three thousand men of the people fell that day. Then Moses said, "You filled your hands to the Lord today, each one on his son or brother, that blessing be given you."

Now it came to pass on the next day that Moses said to the people, "You committed a great sin. So now I will go up to God to make atonement for your sin." Then Moses returned to the Lord and said, "I pray, O Lord, these people have committed a great sin and have made for themselves a god of gold! Yet now, if You will forgive their sin, forgive it—but if not, blot me out of the book You have written." Then the Lord said to Moses, "Whoever sins against Me, I will blot him out of My book. Now therefore, go down and lead the people to the place of which I spoke to you. Behold, My Angel shall go before your face. Nevertheless, in the day when I visit, I will strike them for their sin." So the Lord struck the people for making the calf which Aaron made.

In the Name of the Father, the Son, and the Holy Spirit — One God! Amen.

We give thanks to the Lord our God Who has shown us the way. We give thanks to the Lord who is the Truth, Who is our life, and Who has given us life. Oh, Heavenly Father, send Your Spirit upon us that we indeed might embrace the life that You have given to us. We desire to learn to love the way that You have presented unto us that we might walk worthy of the calling to which we have been called in this day and for the life to come! Amen.

As usual and as is always the case, we want Black lives to matter. We've been talking about this from various aspects of mattering. We've been taking that kaleidoscope and looking down at mattering. We turn it to see mattering from the various angles as it is established and comes to be secured.

We want Black lives to matter, and as we turn that lens today, we want leaders who we can trust to lead us in the right way towards mattering. We want leaders who can lead us to a place where Black lives matter. We want leaders who are not given to us by White power or who White power chooses, and they put out in front of us, and they tell us, "This is your God. This is your leader. This is the one who's going to lead you to freedom. We, your former oppressors know who's going to lead you to the promised land. Here, follow this person." We want leaders who are not seeking notoriety from White power. They may have come up from within us, but what they really want is a pat on the back and a pat at the top of their head from whiteness.

We want leaders who cannot be compromised by White power and who do not see the mattering of Black lives as something needing the agreement of White power or society. Is that what you want from Black leadership in this quest for the mattering of Black lives? What would you say?

How can Black lives matter as a basic fact of life if that mattering is contingent upon the agreement of White power or agreement on whatever ideation we construct about Blackness? We say, "This is what it means to be Black." For it to be valid, it must have validation from White power. How can Black lives matter as a basic fact of life if we always have to wait on, look for, and seek out the agreement of White power on our mattering?

Black lives can only matter by determination between Black people and God. White folks have no say. Asian folks have no say. No one has a say on the essential mattering of Black life except Black people and God, wrong or right?

We would say, "Where are all the leaders?" I hear that all the time. People would say all the time, "We have no leaders. There are no more Martins, no more Malcolms, no more Medgars." People say, "Oh, well where are our leaders? We need new leadership, but where are the leaders?"

If we want Black lives to matter, brothers and sisters, then we want to know where are the leaders, right? "Why are they not presenting themselves?" People would ask me, and say, "Well, where are the leaders? Where are they hiding? Why are they not presenting themselves? Why are they nowhere to be found?"

Why do we, the Black people, continue finding and choosing leaders who lead us back to Egypt? They are leaders who pacify us on behalf of Egypt and who always seem to be in cahoots with Egypt, Babylon, and White power. Why is it that we continuously choose and follow these leaders who aren't leading us to the promised land? You ever ask yourself that question?

We seem to do so because in our hearts, we still desire to be in the land of our oppression. We still desire to be under the authority of White power. That's our problem. We still hold a sweet spot in our hearts for the land of our oppressor. We still see the good in it. There is good in it, and we are willing to concede to the good in it.

We still see Egypt as a land where good has outweighed the bad and the ugly. We see Egypt/Babylon/America as a place where the good of White power has outweighed the bad of White power.

We hold that special place in our hearts for this way of life in the land of our oppression. We prefer leadership that will indulge our unfaithfulness. We prefer leadership that will allow us — even help us — to find virtue in the ways of our oppression and our oppressors. We willingly seek out and choose leaders who will lead us back to Egypt because we don't want to leave. We choose leaders who will lead us back to Egypt mentally, physically, and spiritually.

And this is what we uncover in Exodus Chapter 32. The passage begins by saying, "When the people saw that Moses delayed from coming down the mountain..." The leader, Moses, who had held them accountable was missing. They didn't know where he was. They couldn't find him. "As for this Moses, we don't know what has become of him." They couldn't find him.

"Where are all the leaders?", they cried. "Where are these leaders that You said will lead us? We cannot find them. We cannot see them." He was no longer around. We would say that these kinds of leaders are no longer with us. He was missing, but did they really want to find him?

The Hebrews didn't really want to leave Egypt. They continuously contended with Moses, right? They were always fussing and fighting with Moses. Moses had to pull teeth to get them to come along. They were always trying to go back and constantly proclaimed the glories of Egypt. When they were hungry, they'd look to Moses and say, "Would we had died sitting by the pots of meat and eating bread to the full back in Egypt, man? We would have never thirst back in Egypt. Everybody had water to drink including our livestock and our cattle. Man, Egypt was a great place, but you brought us out here in this desert to die."

They were like, "We didn't want to leave Egypt, and the one who brought us out from the land of Egypt is missing. Let us take this opportunity to go back to Egypt, even if only in our hearts." When they said that to themselves, Pastor Aaron put up absolutely no resistance to the whims of the people. Rather than compel the people to faithfulness as Moses would have done, he immediately gave in to their wrangling. They said, "As for Moses, the man who brought us up from this land of Egypt, we do not know what has become of him." Aaron then said to them, "Remove the gold earrings in the ears of your wives and your daughters, bring them to me." They all removed their earrings and Aaron used them to make a molten calf. Then he said, "These are your gods, O Israel, that brought you out of the land of Egypt."

Pastor Aaron was the one who identified and created the idol and built the altar before the calf. Aaron was the one who led them to worship the calf. Aaron, their pastor and leader, was the one who ushered unfaithfulness into the midst of the people. It was their leader who had set idols before them to worship.

I remember being a pastor at a traditional church. Frankly, I stopped being a pastor to a congregation because parishioners believe that the pastor is there to perform their will. Parishioners believe in their minds that the priest or pastor is there to do the will of the congregation. The judgment and determination of a good priest or pastor is how well that person does what the people want him to do. It may even be how good that pastor is at "spiritually manipulating" the people into thinking they are controlling his ministry. If the priest doesn't do the will of the leading faction in the congregation, that House Targarian will make that pastor's life a living hell.

Maybe it's not you. Maybe it is you, but certainly you know parishioners in the congregations where you attend or have attended.

You know parishioners there who, if the pastor doesn't do their will or live up to their expectations, will take it upon themselves to make that pastor's life a living hell.

We tend to want the leader to lead us in the way that we want to be led. If the leader does not lead the people the way the people want to be led, the people will go out and find another leader. It's like the Israelites who said, "Pastor Moses won't do what we want," so they ran to Pastor Aaron.

They knew Pastor Aaron's character and tendencies. This wasn't the first time. This couldn't have been the first time he acquiesced to their will. They knew Pastor Aaron, and that's why they went to him while Moses was away. They knew that Aaron would appease their unfaithfulness and allow them to hold on to some of their sinfulness.

While Moses endeavored to keep unfaithfulness outside the camp, Aaron had given that unfaithfulness room and life in the midst of the people. The flames of love for the land of their oppression were fanned by Aaron. Their love for the land of their oppression was appeased. Their love for the way that they had learned in the land of their oppression was normalized. However, that love for Egypt that was rooted in the hearts of the Hebrew people and their fondness for the way that they had learned in Egypt had to be consumed and done away with.

In verse nine, the Lord said to Moses, "Now therefore, let Me be, that I may burn in wrath against them and consume them." The Lord had a desire to consume that which was unfaithful and to wipe them out. Ungodliness must be consumed. In verse 20, Moses took the calf that they had made, burned it in a fire, ground it into powder, scattered it on the water, and made the children of Israel drink it.

I tell people my Moses was a big man. Moses made people cower and bow down before him because they were afraid of him. Moses ground that calf into powder, threw it in the water, mixed it up, and made them drink that water. The best visual is from the movie *Friday* when Deebo (RIP Tiny) took the bike from Red and said, "That's my bike, punk!" Moses said, "Drink that water."

The Lord was going to consume them in their ungodliness. In exchange, Moses made the people consume their own ungodliness when he had them drink the calf powder mixture. By this act, Israel overcame its idolatry.

As St. Augustine would say, "Therefore, perhaps this calf being ground to powder was cast into the water and given to the children of Israel to drink so the body of ungodliness might be swallowed up by Israel." Ungodliness had to be consumed, digested, and expelled from the body.

Moses knew this, which is why he demanded faithfulness from his people. On the other hand, Aaron seemed to be unaware that he had to hold the people accountable. So, in verses 21 and 22, Moses said to Aaron, "What did these people do to you that you brought so great a sin upon them?" Aaron replied, "Do not be angry, my lord. You know how impulsive these people are."

Moses said, "Yes, Aaron. Yes. I do know how impulsive the people are," for he had been dealing with them, their impulsivity, and their rebellious desires the entire time. Moses knew how impulsive they were and this was nothing new for him. Moses would tell them, "Why do you contend with me and why do you fight against the Lord your God?" They contended with him repeatedly, but Moses had never acquiesced to their whims. Moses had never made room for their ungodliness, but Aaron did. So, Moses had to cleanse the people from their ungodliness.

Verses 26 through 28 says:

Moses then stood in the entrance of the camp and said, "Whoever is on the Lord's side, come to me." So all the sons of Levi gathered themselves together to him. He said to them, 'Thus says the Lord, God of Israel: "Let every man put his sword on his side and go in and out from entrance to entrance throughout the camp and let every man kill his brother, every man his companion, and every man his neighbor."' So the sons of Levi did as Moses said to them, and about 3000 men of the people fell that day.

Moses cut out the cancer. Moses killed the virus. Moses inoculated the people. Moses removed the plague from the body that they might yet live.

St. Gregory the Great spoke about putting all vices to death and he said:

To go from entrance to entrance is to hasten with rebuke from vice to vice whereby death enters the soul. To pass through the midst of the host is to live with such perfect impartiality within the church as to rebuke the faults of sinners and not to turn aside to favor anyone. Therefore, it is properly added that every man kills his brother and friend and neighbor. That is, a man kills brother and friend and neighbor when, discovering what should be punished, he does not refrain from using the sword of reproof even in the case of those whom he loves for his kinship with them.

Beloved, Moses would not allow the people to hold on to their vice or their unfaithfulness. He would not let them hold on to their sickness. He would not let them preserve any vestige of the way of bondage nor the way of life that they had learned in bondage.

We must entirely reject the ways of Babylon in mind, body, and spirit. We must stop longing for the ways that we learned in Egypt, Babylon, and America. We must come to reject the way that we learned to survive in the land of our oppression. We should not even want that way of life to have anything to do with the life that we are free to live in the promised land and beloved community.

We should not allow how we learned to survive in the land of our suppression to affect the way we live or the liturgy of mattering in the promised land and beloved community. We must reject the comforts that we have learned to find in the land of our oppression.

I was listening to an audiobook by Viktor Frankl called *Man's Search for Meaning.* He talked about the Jews, the Holocaust, and the Holocaust experience and the inhumane treatment that they received in the Nazi concentration camps. While they suffered, they found comfort in certain things and tried to preserve a modicum of humanity by singing, dancing, and finding joy in the midst of their oppression.

We are the same way with hundreds of years of bondage in slavery and Jim Crow segregation. We learn to find comforts and things to help us survive the hellacious experience of life in this land. You know how they say, "When life gives you lemons, you make lemonade." We learned to make lemonade from rotten lemons! We must reject that lemonade...to see freedom as more precious than security, be able to take a leap of faith, take a risk, and venture into the unknown trusting in God alone. The Israelites still longed for the way that they learned in Egypt. It kept them safe for all those hundreds of years.

"Do you mean to tell me that this way of life is bad, wrong, not enough, or not right? This way of life has kept us alive in Egypt for the last 400 years in bondage. Many of our brave ancestors lived this way. They taught us to live this way, and this is the way that we stayed alive thus far. We have come this far by faith."

They weren't going to betray the way that they had learned in the land of their bondage. They would say, "You're not going to tell me that I have to reject that way. We're going to hold firm to that way."

So, when Moses tried to keep them in alignment with a new way, they found a leader who would allow them to hold on to their unfaithfulness.

Brothers and sisters, we Black people must come to desire a new way that was not constructed under the influence of White supremacy. We must desire a way that is free from the limitations that are set by White power and is unlike our current way. Whatever way we have as a people, for as good as it may be, it was constructed under the influence of and in a social space that was limited by White power. The limitations were set by White power. Therefore, the way to the promised land for Black people must be a way that is unlike our current way that has brought us this far, but a way that will at last enable us to overcome.

We must yearn for a way that will not only allow us to see the promised land in the distance from the mountain top but will finally allow us to enter that promised land and live in beloved community. We must begin cultivating a new way, starting from where we are to intentionally change course. We would say, "I don't have time. I have bills to pay. I have this to do. I have that to do."

Everyone's life is just too busy. We are on this hamster wheel, and we cannot stop. Can't stop. Won't stop. COVID had given us all an opportunity to stop and intentionally make a change, but many of us are excited to "return to normal."

The way of life in this society is a way that loves death. It claims to be pro-life while upholding policies that have brought about so much death. We say we don't have time. We don't have time to look at our way of life and change our way of life. We don't have time. I've just got to keep up with the Joneses. Man, I've just got to keep up. COVID slowed us all down and gave us time to reconsider the efficacy of this way that we have been following. This is the way we beheld and continue to hold as critical to our identity as a people. Despite this, we are so grateful to return to normal — to the struggle for mattering and our social lives that have become necessary to help us cope with the realities of our existence.

Reflect on the way you are returning. Has this way of life, liturgy for mattering, and culture that we hold been effective at creating a people? Has this way that we've upheld effectively moved our people into the promised land? Has our way of life manifested the beloved community and the place where Black lives matter as a foundational and fundamental principle?

How did you spend your Passover? The plague came and it's starting to lift. Are you coming out of Passover to return to normal, to life in Egypt as it was before the plague?

We would say that we're too busy to consider these questions, but we had time...you had time. How did you use the time? The Word says that we must be redeeming the time for the days are short. How are you using this time? How are you using the space that has been created?

How have you filled this space that has been created because of shutdowns, lock downs, and slowing of work. How have you healed the space that has been created? Are you even aware of this space? Do you even know that this space exists? Are you aware of what's in this space? Have you taken the time to look at this space and see what it is? Have you been investigating this space? How have you been investigating this space? How have you been seeking to understand this space?

How are you working to get off the hamster wheel? What keeps you on the hamster wheel? What needs to happen over the next three to five years for you to know that you need a new way or a different way? What needs to happen within that time for you to decide to become actively engaged in the process of learning a new way?

Brothers and sisters, we must desire leadership that will hold the way before us and remind us of our true and living God. We need leadership that will remind us of the promise of God, the One who brought us up from slavery. We must have leadership that can keep us desiring and aspiring the promised land while holding us accountable to making it the promised land of beauty that transcends all which we've ever seen and experienced under White power. There must be leadership that is committed to seeing us remain faithful and accountable to the way that leads to the promised land and beloved community. Those leaders must exist. I'm sure they are out there now. The Lord said, "I will never leave you nor forsake you." He said, "I send to you another helper who will be with you always...Lo, I am with you always, even until the end of the age." If He is with us, then the spirit of the Lord is upon someone to proclaim the acceptable year of the Lord and to set the captives free.

Those leaders must exist. They must be out there somewhere, right? We just have to look for that type of leadership and refuse to follow the leaders who do not demand nor inspire excellence.

If you're Black, you should know about HBCU marching bands — even if you haven't been to an HBCU — and how important they are to the life cycle of the community. You should understand that Black musicians choose what school to attend by their choice of the marching band.

They don't choose a school that has a weak band director. They don't choose a school that has a weak band. They want to be in a band that is disciplined. They want to be in a band where the band director demands excellence. No one wants to go to a school where the band is crappy and the band director doesn't care. That's not the school that they want to attend or the program they want to join. Any of you who were athletes or may be athletes know that no one wants to be part of a program where the coach doesn't want to win. Yes, you might have fun. You might score 150 points, but you know you'll never compete for a championship. We know what type of players enjoy such an environment. What type of athlete are you? What type of player are you?

Paul said, "Those who run the race run to win, and if you run, run to win." What kind of coach are you going to look for? What kind of coach do you want to lead you?

You're going to want that coach who keeps you focused on the championship — the promised land — and who keeps you focused on and moving toward the goal. You'll want the coach who won't appease the ways that keep you from being the best that you can be in pursuit of the goal. If you really want freedom from White supremacy and you don't just want to talk about freedom from White supremacy, then acknowledge the need to reject the ways of the oppressor. Acknowledge the need to reject the ways we learned to live that even resembles the good life in the midst of our oppression while under White power.

If you want to be free from White power, you must rid yourself of the ways that you learned made you happy under White power. If you're holding on to the ways that you learned to make you happy or to find peace, you will always remain in subjugation to White power. We must refuse, brothers and sisters, to continue following those who lead us by preventing us from being our best selves. We must refuse to follow those leaders who are not clearly and explicitly committed to seeing us free from subjugation by White power. We must desire to learn a way that is free from the influence of White power, and that is not focused on appeasing genteel White power or fear to protect ourselves from vitriolic White power.

We must desire to learn a true Ubuntu which means *"I am because we are."* It is an identity that is not framed by or under pressure from White power. Rather, it is when little Black boys and Black girls can find themselves and can find the Great I Am within them, because we are. We are a people who know ourselves so we can communicate an ideation of self that is free from the mental, physical, and spiritual baggage that comes with White supremacists and Black inferioricists or Black subjugationist ideology. When we have that way that is free from influence by White power, we can be bequeath to posterity. We can give our children a sense of self that is and can be developed free from the pressures of living under White power. Think about that. Is that not really what we want? Is that not truly the foundation of Black mattering?

May the Lord bless and keep us. May the Lord give us strength and courage to live this life. May He give us strength and courage to embrace the life that He has given unto us that we might not turn to the right nor to the left and that we certainly would not return to Egypt in either our minds, bodies, or spirits! May He give us that diligence and persistence to continue onward and upward toward His holy calling that we might inherit and live in the beloved community. May the blessing of God Almighty, the Father, the Son, and the Holy Spirit be upon you, be with you, strengthen you, and keep you from this day forth and evermore. Amen.

Chapter Nine

Exodus 33:1-11

God Orders Israel to Depart Sinai Now the Lord said to Moses, "Depart, go up from here, you and the people you brought out of the land of Egypt, to the land I swore to Abraham, Isaac, and Jacob, saying, 'To your seed I will give it.' I will send My Angel before your face, and I will drive out the Amorite, the Hittite, the Perizzite, the Gergesite, the Hivite, the Jebusite, and the Canaanite. I will bring you into a land flowing with milk and honey; for I will not go up in your midst, lest I consume you on the way, for you are a stiff-necked people." When the people heard this bad news, they mourned in lamentations. For the Lord said to the children of Israel, "You are a stiff-necked people. Beware, lest I inflict another plague on you and consume you. Now therefore, take off your bright clothes and ornaments, and I will show you what I will do." So the children of Israel stripped themselves of their bright clothes and ornaments by Mount Horeb. Moses before the Lord Moses then took his tent and pitched it outside the camp, far from the camp, and called it the tabernacle of testimony. Thus it came to pass that everyone who sought the Lord went out to the tabernacle of testimony, which was outside the camp. So it was, whenever Moses went out to the tabernacle, which was outside the camp, all the people rose, and each man stood at his tent door and watched Moses until he went into the tabernacle. Now it came to pass, when Moses entered the tabernacle, that the pillar of cloud descended and stood at the door of the tabernacle, and God talked to Moses. All the people saw the pillar of cloud standing at the tabernacle door, and all the people rose and worshiped, each man at his tent door. Thus the Lord spoke to Moses face to face, as a man speaks to his friend. Then he would return to the camp, but his servant Joshua the son of Nun, a young man, did not depart from the tabernacle.

In the name of the Father, the Son, and the Holy Spirit — One God! Amen.

Heavenly Father, we give thanks to you for your love and your guidance that never leave nor forsake us. We give thanks to the Lord, our God, for His hand of favor, His hand of deliverance, and His hand of blessing. We give thanks to You, oh Lord, for being patient and remaining with us, even if outside the camp, as we come to decide that we want you in our lives. May the Lord give us strength and courage to welcome Him into the camp that we might be confronted by His grace and love so that we can walk worthy of the calling to which we have been called. We desire to make it in this journey towards the promised land and his beloved community. Amen.

It's good to be with you all. I pray that the Lord has been good to you and that you are experiencing His revelation in your life. I pray that things are becoming more and more clear and that you are receiving more peace and joy. May you be enveloped by more and more love.

Again, we've been looking at making Black lives matter. This has been the overarching and prevailing theme that has been "in your face" for the past centuries, but it's really been smacking you in the face for the past few years. This desire and need for Black lives to matter is what we want more than anything. We want to have a foundational mattering that is not conditioned by the need for benevolence from those who have historically behaved malevolently.

We want a foundational and essential mattering that is not dependent upon the need for good actions or intentions from those who have not historically had the best intentions. We want a mattering that does not depend upon White power.

In other words, we want a mattering. We want to matter at the very center of our being. Mattering must happen at the core of our being as human beings and at the core of our identity. We want a mattering that is unchangeable, unequivocal, unshakable and that does not change because the president changed. We long for a mattering that does not change because the state of the economy has changed or because whatever social, environmental, or economic machinations have happened. We want a mattering that has substance and is steadfast, no matter the political or economic times.

We want the mattering that is central to our identity and foundational to who we are and how we see ourselves, but we really don't want the Lord too close. We don't want God "too close," but we want Him close enough.

"Nearer to thee, oh Lord!" We want Him close, but we don't want Him too close. We want Him close enough that He is there when we want Him, but we want Him far enough to keep Him from disturbing our way of life.

The Lord is annoying to us. No one will like me saying that, but the Lord is annoying to us. God gets on our nerves confronting us with our unfaithfulness all the time and demanding our accountability to the way. He always reminds us of why we should be grateful to Him. None of you want the Lord always nagging you and reminding you of how you're wrong or how the way that you've come to cherish is no longer "the way." The Lord is annoying to us.

So, we have cast the Lord out of our camp. We've allowed Him to remain outside. He can stay out there. He can hang out on the sidelines. We've continued to reject Him. There's nothing new about that. You see, the Lord was annoying to the Hebrew people too.

That's what we see in Exodus 33:1-11. This was immediately after they had constructed the golden calf. Remember, we previously discussed how they constructed the golden calf. Moses came back, and he had to do penance for them. He pleaded with the Lord for them and tried to save them. He sacrificed some of them, and then he made atonement.

They had committed the ultimate affront to God by making the golden calf. In Exodus 33, we see how the Lord responded.

Now, the Lord said to Moses, "Depart, go up from here, you and the people you brought out of the land of Egypt to the land I swore to Abraham, Isaac, and Jacob saying to your seed, I will give it. I will send my angel before your face and I will drive out the Amorite, the Hittite, the Perizzite, the Gergesite, the Hivite, the Jebusite, and the Canaanite. I will bring you into a land flowing with milk and honey; for I will not go up in your midst lest I consume you on the way, for you are a stiff-necked people. When the people heard this bad news, they mourned in lamentations. For the Lord said to the children of Israel, "You are a stiff-necked people. Beware, lest I inflict another plague on you and consume you. Now, therefore take off your bright clothes and ornaments, and I will show you what I will do." So, the children of Israel stripped themselves of their bright clothes and ornaments by Mount Horeb.

Moses then took his tent and pitched it outside the camp, far from the camp, and called it the tabernacle of testimony. Thus, it came to pass that everyone who sought the Lord went out to the tabernacle of testimony, which was outside the camp. So it was, whenever Moses went out to the tabernacle, which was outside the camp, all the people rose, and each man stood at his tent door and watched Moses until he went into the tabernacle. Now, it came to pass, when Moses entered the tabernacle that the pillar of cloud descended and stood at the door of the tabernacle and God talked to Moses.

All the people saw the pillar of cloud standing at the tabernacle door, and all the people rose and worshiped each man at his tent door. Thus the Lord spoke to Moses face to face as a man speaks to his friend. Then he would return to the camp, but his servant Joshua the son of Nun, a young man did not depart from the tabernacle.

Back in chapter 32, the Lord said to Moses:

Go quickly. Get down from here for your people whom you brought out of the land of Egypt are transgressing the law. They turned aside quickly from the way I commanded them. They made themselves a calf and are worshiping and sacrificing to it and are saying, "These are your gods, oh, Israel that brought you out the land of Egypt. Now, therefore, let me be that I may burden our wrath against them and consume them. Then I will make of you a great nation.

The Lord was just like, "Let me at them. Let me at them you little ungrateful so and so's."

Moses had tried to make amends, and he pleaded before God. He went back down to the people. He ground that calf into powder, made a mixture, and drank it. He sacrificed more than 3,000 people then went again to make atonement to the Lord. He understood the magnitude of what they had done to the Lord and the magnitude of gratitude, ungratefulness, and of their sacrilege and blasphemy. He went again to make atonement for the people.

In Chapter 32, Verse 33, we see the response that he got from the Lord.

Then the Lord said to Moses, whoever sins against me, I will blot him out of my book. Now, therefore, go down and lead the people to the place of which I spoke to you. Behold, my angel shall go before your face. Nevertheless, in the day when I visit, I will strike them for their sin. So the Lord struck the people for making the calf, which Aaron made.

Now see, brothers and sisters, the people had rejected God and Moses, the servant of God, who was striving to hold them accountable to the way. They did not want to follow the way. They preferred the way that they had learned in Egypt.

They wanted to receive the promises of God and the land of milk and honey, but they did not want him to disturb their way of life. They wanted the benefits of the Lord without offering their obedience to His way. In response, God promised not to leave them. "I ain't going no place. I'm going to love you because I said I'm going to love you, and that's who I am. I am the same yesterday, today, and forever. I'm going to love you. I ain't going no place." God promised not to leave them.

He went outside the camp so that they could be who they wanted to be. He was not going to force them to embrace Him. He was not going to force them to embrace His way. If they wanted to come to Him at the tabernacle of testimony, they could come. He was out there for them to come. If they wanted him to stay out from their midst, He would stay out lest He consume them, for they were a stiff-necked people. The Lord said, "You know what? These people are so stiff-necked. It's better if I just stay out from among them because if I come among them, I'm going to slaughter every last one of them. It's better for them, because I love them, and I don't want to destroy them. It's better for them if I grant them their wish, and I just back off."

The people had cast God out of their camp. And the word says, "Oh, they lamented when the people heard this bad news, they mourned in lamentations." They lamented because the Lord had called them a stiff-necked people. They lamented, but they never repented. They never acknowledged their rejection of God. They never cleaned up the camp and made a place for the Lord to return to their midst. They never came out to the Lord outside the camp and expressed their desire to have Him as the center of their lives, their community, and of who they were as a people.

Back in Exodus chapter 20, verse 21, the Lord spoke to Moses after he came down from the mountain. Verse 19 says, "Then they said to Moses, "Speak with us and we will hear; but let not God speak with us lest we die." We don't want to hear from Him. The people stood afar off, but Moses drew near the thick darkness where God was. The people didn't want to be too close. They stood afar off. They were like, "Nah, we don't want Him too close because He is going to upset my way of life. He's going to upset my way of being. He will tell me about myself, and He will make me become something that I don't want to be. I want Him to free me, but I don't want Him too close. I'm going to hold Him at bay so that I can be who I really want to be."

The people stood afar off, but Moses drew near. They never wanted to get close to God. The people finally got their wish, and God kept His distance from them. The people were sad that the Lord had gone outside of the camp. The people were sad. They lamented that He was no longer at the center of their lives as a people and that their relationship with Him was no longer central to their identity, but they never repented of their way. This made it clear to the Lord that His presence was not what they had desired most.

In Exodus 33, verse seven, Moses took his tent and pitched it outside the camp, far from the camp, and called it a tabernacle of testimony. He took his tent where he was staying. Thus, it came to pass that everyone who saw the Lord went out to the tabernacle of testimony outside the camp. The tabernacle of testimony is the place where reminders of the Lord's presence and of His blessing were kept.

The tabernacle is a testimony to the Lord's greatness and His goodness. It is a reminder of what the Lord has done for you, His presence in your midst, and His blessings in your life where the Lord's presence is kept. That's the first church. We keep him outside of our homes and outside of our communities in a place where He's isolated. We see him when we want to see him, and when we don't want to see Him, we stay away.

When the people wanted to hear of the Lord's blessing, they went to the tabernacle of testimony. When they wanted to be reminded of His presence in their midst, they went through the tabernacle of testimony. However, when the people did not want to be disturbed by the presence of the Lord, they stayed inside the camp, and they left the Lord outside the camp. As they were becoming a people, this is what they were doing, and this is how they were living. This was how they were thinking and how they behaved. This is how they were developing their identity and establishing their mattering as a people.

In this phase of the establishment of their mattering, the Hebrew people decided that they would define themselves without the Lord in their center. Brothers and sisters, the mattering of a people is found in what lies at its center. The mattering of a people is found in what is at its core. What is at the core of that people? What are the core beliefs of a people? The core beliefs of a people determine their identity.

What's on the periphery of being? What's on the periphery of self? What's on the periphery of one's existence and one's life may shape one's identity. The foundation of that identity is the core — the center. In architecture, you might say that it is the cornerstone or the chief foundation on which something is constructed or developed. The cornerstone, that stone which the builders rejected, has become the chief cornerstone. The builders are the architects of society. In the case of the Hebrew people, the Egyptians were the builders and the architects of their society. The Hebrew people and their slave labor might have built the building, but the architects of the society were the Egyptians — White power. The Stone which the builders rejected had become the Chief Cornerstone. The Stone was rejected by White power and the Egyptians. They did not establish their society with God as the foundation. They may say, "In God, we trust," but by their fruits, you shall know that they are his disciples. By their fruit, we shall know that they have not put God at the center of their society.

That rejected Stone has become the Chief Cornerstone of the people of God. Frankly, it's become that chief cornerstone because it was rejected by the builders the people had learned to reject. It's as if you see the builders who have built a society that breeds a love of death, and you're like, "I want no parts of that." Then, you see that the cornerstone has been rejected, but we must embrace the cornerstone. We want something that is completely and diametrically opposed to the society that they have constructed.

The foundation of something that is completely unlike what they have constructed is founded upon the cornerstone that they have rejected. So, that is why the Stone which the builders rejected has become the Chief Cornerstone for the people of God. It is because that is the Stone that was rejected by the builders. If it was rejected by the builders and the builders created this society, then there must be something in that rejected cornerstone that we definitely want. We want to embrace the rejected cornerstone as part of rejecting the ways that they learned from the builders.

But you see, the Hebrew people wanted to keep the way that they had learned from the builders. They wanted to keep the way that they had learned under Egyptian supervision and authority. They wanted to keep those ways and beliefs that they had developed under Egyptian bondage as their center. These were the beliefs and the ways of life that they had held central to their identity and that made them a people. These are the beliefs and the ways of life that were drawn up for them by the builders of Egyptian society.

These beliefs remained the cornerstone for Hebrew identity. Therefore, they were literally troubled at their core with God in their midst. His presence in their midst confronted them at every turn. Every time they wanted to live according to the cherished way that had carried them through in their sojourn of Egypt and every time they wanted to celebrate some of the old ways that they had learned and that had preserved them, there was the Lord. He was there reminding them of his way and demanding their obedience. He would never just "let them live."

Unlike the Israelites, Moses desired intimacy with God as shown in the Book of Exodus, chapter 33, verses 12 through 23.

Exodus 33 says:

Then Moses said to the Lord, "Behold, you say to me, bring up this people, but you have not let me know whom you will send with me.

Yet you have said, "I know you above all. And you have also found grace in my sight." Now, therefore, I pray. If I have found grace in your sight, reveal yourself to me, that I may see you clearly and find grace in your sight, and know this great nation is Your people.

So, He said, "I myself will go before you and give you rest." No worries. Then he said to Him, "If You Yourself do not go up with us, do not bring us up from here. For how then will it be known that Your people and I have found grace in your sight, except you go with us?" How can it be said that we are Your people and that we have found favor with you? How can it be said that we indeed matter when we were once slaves and told that we were nothing but slaves. How can we matter when, for more than 400 years, we have grown into this identity of slaves and have developed this slave mentality? "How shall we ever know that we are Your people, that we have found grace in Your sight, except You go with us? So, both I and Your people shall be glorified beyond all the nations on the earth."

The Lord said to Moses:

I will also do this thing you have spoken, for you have found grace in my sight, and I know you above all." Moses replied, "Reveal yourself to me." Then God said, "I will pass before you in my glory. And I will proclaim my name, the Lord before you. I will have mercy on whom I will have mercy, and I will have compassion on whom I have compassion." But He said, "You cannot see my face for no man can see my face and live." Moreover, the Lord said, "Here is a place by me. You shall stand on the rock. So it shall be, while my glory passes by it, that I will put you in the cleft of the rock and will cover you with my hand while I pass by. Then I will take away my hand and you shall see my back, but my face shall not be seen.

People long to see the face of the Lord. People long to see what it is they worship — Who it is they worship. You hear it said all the time, "Man, where do you see Christ in the world? I don't see Christ in the world." They may also say, "I see Jesus here, and I see Jesus there." People want to see who it is they worship. Peter Chrysologus, one of the holy fathers said:

This is why love, which longs to see God, even if it lacks judgment, does have the spirit of devotion. This is why Moses dares to say, 'If I have found favor in your sight, show me your face.' This is why another man says, 'Show us your face,' and finally, this is why the Gentiles fashioned idols in their errors. They wanted to see with their eyes, what they were worshiping.

Moses said, "Now, therefore I pray. If I have found grace in Your sight, reveal Yourself to me, that I may see you clearly and find grace in Your sight and know this great nation is Your people." I will know I matter, not because the Egyptians tell me so, but I will know I matter because I see you. If I see you, how could I not matter? For you, oh Lord, God Almighty, wouldn't show yourself to someone who does not matter or a being that has no value. So let me see you, that I may indeed know that I matter, that I have life, and that I have being. Seeing God is what Moses needed to know that he and the Hebrew people "mattered."

Brothers and sisters, when I think on us as Black people, we must desire intimacy with God, rather than intimacy with White people, White society, and White power. We must desire closeness to God rather than — not even more than — desiring closeness to White people. Right now, that's what we want. We want them to love us. We want them to like us. We want them to be nice to us. We want closeness with them. We want them to accept us into their neighborhoods, into their schools, and into their establishments. We want to be close to them, rather than desiring to be close to the One who had freed us from them.

We must desire intimacy with God, rather than intimacy with White society. We must not be satisfied with a mere easing of our condition, our struggle, or our plight. We must realize that the Lord did not free us so that we might simply have conditions that were more easily tolerable. The Lord freed us, that we might have intimacy with Him, like Moses had intimacy with Him.

Moses desired to be one with God. Moses desired to be in the presence of God. It's why Moses took his tent. The people had rejected the Lord. The Lord said, "You are stiff-necked people, and, man, I'm done. I'm going from here." And Moses was like, "Hey, I'm going too." Moses took up his tent, pitched it far outside the camp, and called it a tabernacle of testimony.

Moses stayed at the tabernacle of testimony. Because he still loved the people, Moses returned to the people when they sought intimacy with God. Yet, absent from everything else, his dwelling was in the darkness where God was so that he could rest solely in the presence of God.

I was listening to one of those metaphysician philosopher types, Alan Watts. He gave an analogy to help explain darkness and nothingness. He said that your eyes have a field of vision that's made like an oval and you can see as far as your periphery allows. He said, "What is the color of things beyond your field of vision?" The color of things beyond your field of vision is not Black. The color is no color. There is nothing beyond your field of vision. It is no vision. It is no color.

That is the darkness that we are talking about that Moses entered. This was the place where he completely melted away. All that existed was the presence of the Lord. Like John the Baptist said, Moses desired to " decrease that He might increase." Moses desired to be in that void where he was brought to nothingness and all that existed was God.

When the Lord first sent Moses to free the people, He said, "Free the people that they might come and worship Me on this mountain, that you might be free in God, not be free from God." Moses desired that intimacy with God. He was free, and he wanted to be one with God. There was nothing more precious or sacred to him—nothing. The way that he had learned was not important. What was important was being one with God, being at one with God, and being in intimate relationship with God.

Beloved, we must desire the Lord in our midst more than we desire to be free from His confrontation of our way of life. Yes, the Lord confronts your way of life. There's things that you want to do and have learned to do in this sojourn in Babylon that you enjoy. They are not only luxuries, but also frivolities.

Two thirds of America's economy is built on services. When you look at the economy in this COVID crisis, the impact on services is one thing that is significantly hurting the economy. A vast majority of those who work in services work in the culinary, hospitality, and travel industries, and they are not stable right now.

Still, we want to hold on to this way of life. This way of life is changing, but we struggle. Although everything is telling us that this way of life is changing, and must change, we are still trying to hold on to what we know and what is familiar. We can't let go. We can't let go of the ways that we have learned in this land of our oppression.

So, we cast the Lord out from among us. We tell the Lord, "We're going to keep you in the church. We're going to build a building for you outside of our neighborhoods." Most people don't even go to church in their neighborhood anymore. "We're going to go put You in a building and a tabernacle of testimony outside of our camp, outside of our neighborhood, away from our sphere, and certainly outside of our home. Then, we'll come and visit You when we remember Your blessing. When life gets so hard that we forget about Your blessing and Your presence with us, then we will come to You and get the reminder. However, you stay where you are because we don't really want the Lord telling us about our ways that we've learned in Babylon. We don't want the Lord to confront us with how these ways keep us worshiping White power and keep us in bondage to whiteness.

If we want to be free, we must desire the Lord in our midst. If we want to matter in a way that is rooted in the One who is unchangeable, unshakeable, and is the same yesterday, today and forever, then we must put the Lord at the center of our identity. We must welcome Him back into the camp. We must repent for how we rejected Him and cast Him outside of the camp just so that we could keep what we love in, about, and from the land of our oppression.

We should desire to hold on to the Lord rather than the way of life that we acquired under the influence of White power. We must invite the Lord back into the camp and acknowledge how we cast Him out. Then, we must stop simply lamenting the absence of His presence and start repenting for telling Him that He is not welcome among us. We need to stop saying, "Oh, when will the Lord come? I wish the Lord would deliver us! Jesus come and help us." We must repent for expecting His grace while being unwilling to abandon our way to embrace His way.

We must refocus our gratitude on the One who alone is responsible for our mattering and not those who may or may not vote the right ways, pass the right laws, or whatever the case may be. We must seek a relationship with the Lord that removes us from submission to White authority. The Bible says:

For He is the Lord, your God, who brought you out of the land of Egypt, out of the house of bondage. You shall have no other gods before him. You shall not bow down to them or serve them. For the Lord your God is a jealous God, recompensing the sins of the fathers on the children, unto the third and fourth generation, for those who hate Him, but showing mercy to the thousands, to those who love Him and keep His commandments.

Brothers and sisters, we must make this repentance more than just a statement. In doing so, what is the single greatest fear you feel we, as a people, have that prevents us from abandoning the way that we learned under White supervision? What is the single greatest question you have about how you can begin reshaping your way of life to be free from the limitations of White power? How do you begin? The Lord is going to confront us, and thanks be to God.

We know the suffering that is part of this way which are rooted in White supremacy. We should want our way of life to have nothing to do with that way of suffering and death. We should want to be sure that our way of life has been purged of all filth that has caused such great degradation in the human and humanity in the imago Dei.

Shouldn't we want to be sure? Some say that after the Holocaust, the Jews said, "Never again." We don't ever want to see this happen to anyone else because no people should ever be degraded in the way that we've experienced. Never again should anyone created in the image of God be subjugated to such tyranny, terrorism, and degradation as has been suffered under White power.

Shouldn't we want to make sure that our way of life has nothing to do with White power and that we have rejected the cornerstone of their society to embrace the Chief Cornerstone who is our Lord and Savior, Jesus Christ? How can we matter if our identity is built upon something else? It ain't easy.

May the Lord give us strength and courage that we might determine to walk worthy of the calling to which we have been called. With praise and thanksgiving, let us give thanks to the Lord, our God Who has freed us, redeemed us, and made us His people. Let us embrace Him in the fullness of His being and keep Him as the center of our lives and our identity that we might see who we are to become. May the blessing of God Almighty, the Father, the Son, and the Holy Spirit be upon you and remain with you this day and ever more! Amen.

Conclusion

Ephesians 4:11-17

And He Himself gave some to be apostles, some prophets, some evangelists, and some pastors and teachers, for the equipping of the saints for the work of ministry, for the edifying of the body of Christ, till we all come to the unity of the faith and of the knowledge of the Son of God, to a perfect man, to the measure of the stature of the fullness of Christ; that we should no longer be children, tossed to and fro and carried about with every wind of doctrine, by the trickery of men, in the cunning craftiness of deceitful plotting, but, speaking the truth in love, may grow up in all things into Him who is the head—Christ— from whom the whole body, joined and knit together by what every joint supplies, according to the effective working by which every part does its share, causes growth of the body for the edifying of itself in love. The New Man This I say, therefore, and testify in the Lord, that you should no longer walk as the rest of the Gentiles walk, in the futility of their mind,

In the name of the Father, the Son, and the Holy Spirit — One God! Amen.

We give thanks to You, Lord our God, for Your love and Your blessing in our lives. We give thanks to you, oh Lord, for a new year of life that we can yet again, with Your Word made flesh within us, walk worthy of the calling to which we have been called. Lord God, guide us and protect us along this way that we might find our way along this journey into your promised land! Amen.

Blessings, beloved. Blessings.

We are a people who are serious and intentional about our Christian faith. When we talk about the mattering of Black life, we are really looking for an authentic Christian witness that is void from the justifications of human degradation. Everybody knows that Western (White) Christianity has made all kinds of excuses and rationales for the enslavement of people, stealing their land, and the degradation of humanity. All these things and other heinous acts have been seen as dutiful Christian acts and done in the name of Christ and on behalf of the Kingdom. That is their interpretation of the Faith. Their Christian witness has made justifications for the degradation of humans and humanity. Somehow, they have reconciled that.

What we are looking for is a Christian witness and Christianity that is free from the baggage of White supremacy. The problem that I see is that we don't really understand what that means. We'll say, "I want a faith that is free from White supremacy. I want to extricate and remove any vestige of White supremacy from my faith. I want to remove anything that they have installed in the Faith to twist it to their own devices. I want to construct a Christian faith that is void of that for myself and my family." We can say this, and we can understand it in an abstract, esoteric, semantic sense. We understand it as words, and we understand it intellectually in our minds. I say this because I know that I did too. I understood it in my mind.

The problem is that we don't really know what that means from a tangible perspective. What does that mean? I have to be intentional to say, "Oh, Black Jesus. I pray to you." Do you know what I mean? It's like, "In the name of the Father of African people." What does that really mean? What are we really saying when we talk about constructing a Christian faith that is free from the baggage of White supremacy? We don't really see how this is possible. We don't see the need or the role for the idea of studying theology.

We hear that Western Christianity is supremacist and has been tainted by White supremacy. Western Christianity and White supremacy joined together in unholy matrimony along with their offspring comprised Western civilization. The doctrine of discovery, Dum Diversas, and the other papal bulls laid the groundwork for colonialism. We know about the church's involvement in owning and selling slaves and making justifications for slavery and colonialism. We know all these things. So, we tend to say, "I don't want to be bothered with that. I don't want to be bothered with the theology of what they really believe about predestination, transmutation, and those types of things. All I want is Jesus. Just give me Jesus, and I'm good."

The sense is, "I've identified Jesus; I see Him, and that's what I came for. I'm not worried about the rest of this stuff or this theological mumbo jumbo. Theology is for you people up in the rafters. For me, just give me Jesus. Give me Jesus." We don't see the purpose of studying theology or philosophy to understand what it is that we really believe in this faith. Like the Lord says, "By your fruit shall they know that you are my disciples." So, we don't see the purpose in examining the fruit of these people to understand what it is they believe.

I want to propose to you the idea that once you understand how Western Christianity conceives of the Holy One, you will be compelled to break free from their conception. We assume that while the Black Church might be stylistically different from the White Church, we believe like they believe. Because we think we believe in the same God, we let them teach us. We let them tell us about the Faith. We let them proclaim the Gospel to us, and we let them shape the framework and structures of belief because "we all believe in Jesus." We all believe in God. We hear the White church say, "We believe in one God, Father, Son, and Holy Spirit." Since we say that too, we are all on the same page. We believe. Somehow, we have reconciled that it manifests differently, and that different manifestation is of no consequence.

We see White Christianity lives a Christian faith that allows them to kill people and steal their land while somehow, we are all one. We think that their conception of the Divine, their understanding of the Holy One, and their interpretation of Jesus Christ is the same as ours.

I would say that the purpose of studying theology and philosophy is to see what they are saying about "XYZ." I believe that once you understand how Western Christianity conceives of the Holy One, you would be convicted and compelled to break free of their conception.

When I examine what they believe about Christian concepts like Christ and His oneness, the Trinity, the Old and New Testament, and Judeo-Christianity, I'm like, "Oh man, I don't want anything to do with this. This cannot be right. You can't get into the kingdom of God believing these things."

When I came to understand how Western Christians conceptualize the Divine and their relationship with Him, I was compelled to break free from their conception. Breaking free from the conception will shift you from simply talking about it to constructing a liturgy of life in the Christian faith that is nothing like the Christianity given to you by our oppressors, the deceivers.

A lot of Paul's work was about rooting out deceivers who were coming among the people and telling them that they could live a different kind of Christianity. That's why we're in Ephesians 4:11-17.

In the latter part of the passage it says, "You should no longer walk as the rest of the Gentiles walk, in the futility of their mind." This means to understand that their interpretations are useless to us.

What is your mind telling you? What is your gut telling you in this moment when you read that Paul said we should no longer be, "Children tossed to and fro and carried about with every wind of doctrine by the trickery of men, in the cunning craftiness of deceitful plotting?" What was more deceitful and plotting than White supremacy and the Western Church partnering with the ideological fathers and mothers of White supremacy?

They constructed a deceitful plot in the craftiness and cunning of men to find ways to rule and conquer the world in the name of whiteness. However, they said it was in the name of Jesus and that they were spreading the gospel to Christianize savages.

I know it's hard for us as Black folks to listen to other Blacks say this kind of stuff. Robert P. Jones wrote a book called *White Too Long* and detailed a statistical analysis of White Christian culture. As part of his research, he created a racism index with a list of questions to determine the scale from one to 10 to which someone is a racist. A score of 10 was the most racist.

He said that White evangelicals such as White mainline Christians, Protestants, Catholics, Methodists, and Episcopalians scored an eight out of 10 on this scale. Lutherans and others scored a seven out of 10 as racist. People tend to believe that Evangelicals are the racist ones. The Episcopalians typically have a Black presiding Bishop, so they ain't racist—but they still scored a seven out of 10.

In an interview, Jones also said, "So now, help me understand. Are you talking about Christians in name only, or people who go to church?" He said they controlled for that. They wanted to see if there was a difference between those who claimed to be Christian but didn't go to church and those who religiously went to church. For the mainline denominations, the score did not change. The score also didn't change for Catholics, Anglicans, Episcopalians, Methodists, or Lutherans. If you went to church or not, your score was still a seven out of 10.

Jones suggested that the evangelicals were better off if they did not go to church because the more they went to church, the more racist they tended to be. Non-Christian Whites scored best; they were the least racist. They scored a four out of 10. Essentially, he found that the more Christian you are in this country, the more likely you are to be racist. In other words, racism and White supremacy are taught through Western Christianity, especially through American Christianity. It teaches and inculcates White supremacy, which also means that it reinforces Black inferiority.

This is why Stephanie Spellers, a Black female who serves as Canon for Reconciliation to the Black man who serves as Presiding Bishop of the Episcopal Church, said to me, "A strong Black identity has no place in the Episcopal Church." Western Christianity inculcates White supremacy and Black inferiority.

Once you understand how Western Christianity conceives of the Holy One, understanding the building blocks of faith can be taken seriously. Theological concepts like Christology, pneumatology (the theology of the spirit), and Mariology (the theology of Mary and the doctrine of the Trinity) are all building blocks of our faith. You don't need to worry about these now, but they are doing what they were intended to do which is to indoctrinate you with White supremacist and Black inferioricist thoughts.

Brothers and sisters, we must begin to construct a faith that is liberated from White supremacy which will also liberate us from White supremacy. Even if we don't pay much attention, or we aren't religious in our practice, our faith guides our lives. You understand that, right? Our faith and what we believe about life guides our lives. When we believe something long enough, we don't need to worry about what we are believing.

When you get to a cruising altitude with no turbulence, you switch on the autopilot. "You're now free to walk around the cabin." On autopilot, you go your own way, and that's where we have been. I'm not saying there's anything wrong with going on autopilot. What is wrong is that we have been on autopilot with the building blocks that were given to us by our oppressors thinking that we are going to arrive at the destination that we intended.

A faith that has not been liberated from White supremacy cannot liberate you from White supremacy. For you to be free, get from under the thumb, or from under the knee of White subjugation that is on our necks, your faith must be liberated.

To truly become beloved community, we must be liberated from White supremacy and extricate it from ourselves, our families, and our communities to create that place where Black lives matter on earth as it is in heaven. We know that Black lives matter in heaven, right? We just take that as a given; we know that. We also say, "Thy Kingdom come on earth as it is in heaven." In heaven, Black lives matter, so that means on earth Black lives must come to matter.

When Black lives matter on earth as it is in heaven, we can construct a Christian faith that has been liberated from White supremacy and is then able to liberate us from White supremacy. We must allow space to truly become beloved community where love, peace, joy, and oneness rule the day. The place where Black lives matter is one where little Black boys and Black girls can grow up without a diminished sense of self or wonder who they are in this world because the world tells them that they have no value merely because of the color of their skin.

How does that aspirational goal sound to you? What do you think about when I refer to examining and intentionally choosing building blocks of faith to construct the temple of your soul which is your faith? Think about it. We were all given faiths. They were passed down to us. Very few of us have strayed from the faith that we have been given nor have we had to learn a new faith. We may have strayed from being Baptist to become AME or from being Christian Methodists, Christian Episcopalians, or CME to become Baptist or something else. We may have changed our faith in that way.

For the most part, you're still a Christian if you were born a Christian. It may also be that you have no faith to hold. Therefore, all we did was possibly learn the "on the ground living" of the faith. We never learned the building blocks of faith because they were all just passed down to us from generation to generation. We've never had to pick them up and examine them to determine if we really wanted to build our house upon them? Is this the true foundation? Is this a firm foundation on which to build my house?

We must actually be about examining those building blocks. We must really criticize and analyze what composes our faith. What is that thing? What things do we want? How should we be using those blocks? How should those blocks fit together for us to construct an identity that is indeed liberative and will restore us to the imago Dei and the fullness of our Blackness?

Do you believe that we must construct a faith or a Christian identity that conceives of God whose will is to liberate Black people from the subjugation by White power and whose will is for Black lives to matter?

The thing is that I can't make you do it; you have to want to do it. You must want to have that sort of faith. You must believe that your faith is critical to your freedom and that your faith will be the thing that undergirds your freedom into the promised land. I know that we talk about wanting freedom, but you have to believe that your faith has a foundational, critical role in that journey. If so, then you want to create a faith that can liberate you from White supremacy. Over time, this faith will liberate you in thought, word, and deed so that you can function on a new level where you are not impacted by White supremacy because your faith will create an anti-White supremacist force field against it.

We talk about the beloved community as a place where Black lives matter. We see this place in our mind's eye. When we can really envision it and if this place becomes real for you, there is a particular type of faith that is becoming of that place, right? Certain ways of life could not exist in the beloved community. Do you know what I mean? This is not just racism, but lying, cheating, stealing, and those kinds of things cannot exist and is not becoming in the beloved community. When we talk about becoming beloved community, we should also be talking about developing a faith and walking in a way that is becoming of beloved community, right?

When we talk about philosophy of religion, we're referring to the way people bind themselves back to the God Who they conceive of. So, there's multiple ways to say that, right? Religion is the way that people bind themselves to God. It is also the way that they conceive of God and how they conceive of binding themselves to God. For better or for worse, we want to be connected to the source of power. That's what White power is all about. They want to take the power of God. This is exactly what Bonhoeffer would say, "Humanity sicut deus, humanity like God." It is exactly the fall of creation where humanity acquires the knowledge of good and evil and no longer needs God because they are supreme — White supremacy. They no longer need God because they are over and above God. They call on God like a genie.

Before we do intentional work, we must recognize that we all have a faith where some things just have to be excused away. For example, "The Christian church justified slavery." You can't excuse that away. The church justified slavery. Consequently, you must come up with some excuse so that reality doesn't matter. You don't have a theological framework to show that this was a heretical move that declares them not to be Christian. You can only excuse that away like it didn't happen and like it doesn't matter.

We want to construct a faith where your children won't turn to you and say, "Well, why do you believe that?", and you don't have an answer. Or worse, you respond, "That's just what we believe."

No, no, no. When your children ask you, you should have an answer and be able to tell them exactly why you believe it and where it comes from. When they struggle to understand what they see in this

Western world that is masquerading as Christianity then they come to you to tell you about it, you can help them understand how that is not Christianity. When you can really conceive of and understand a faith that is yours, you won't respond to your children by saying things like, "Oh, we don't do that in this house."

When I think about 2021, I start where we began. 2020 was a year. I told people, "Hey, I wouldn't be surprised if it snows this year in Florida. The way 2020 has been going, I would not rule out snow." We didn't get snow, but one day it was 20-something degrees here so we got close. It could have snowed. 2020 was a year and not just because of COVID, but it was all the things that COVID brought. For me, it was even things that were influenced by COVID, but were waiting to happen anyway. 2020 was a year of piling on.

The solace that I take is captured by this experience. I was recently spreading some compost around my yard, and that ain't nothing but waste too. It's filth and poop, but when that poop gets spread on the ground, it makes the ground fertile. If the mix isn't right, you have to add some more poop. Once the ground has been covered in enough poop, the soil becomes fertile and good fruit grows.

When I think on 2021 and all the filth and poop that has been sprinkled upon us in 2020 and in years past, I give thanks to God because what man meant for evil, God used for good. The poop in my life and in your life can be the beginnings of fertile soil for the fruit to be harvested this year.

So, as we talk about the mattering of Black lives entering the promised land where Black lives matter, I believe that this year is a year we've got to be about building that faith that enables us to walk worthy of freedom….and that work is deep work. It's work.

That's what the West does as well; they teach you that work is bad so that no one wants to do any work. We can't wait for the weekend so that we don't have to work because nobody is doing work that they want to do. We're all doing work that we have to do. Yes, we have to do this work, but by God's grace, we will want to do this work too because we want to be free. Do you want to be free, or do you just want to talk about being free?

If we want to be free, then it's going to take work and that should be work that we are delighted to do. You may wonder why I'm talking about this work. Well, it's a blessed and a holy work because that work will set you and your family up for generations to come, enabling you to live a life that is free from White subjugation, beyond the reach of White supremacy, and is becoming of beloved community. You were destined to walk worthy of the calling to which you have been called and to look forward to the kingdom that is to come because you have experienced and lived in it.

So, I hope you take the time to fill out a survey at JahBread.com/philosophy. I would really appreciate it. If any of you are at a loss for how to get started, I'll leave this page open for you to connect with me. By God's grace, I'll help you get started.

Like I said, we're in this together. So, I make myself available to you at JahBread.com/philosophy. In the meantime, remember to connect with me on social media if you have any questions. You can find me on Instagram, Twitter, YouTube, and Facebook.

Well, brothers and sisters, I give thanks for the time to be with you, to share this space with you, and to share the Word with you. May the Lord comfort and guide you in 2021 and beyond that you might find your way into the promised land. May He fill your heart with joy and your life with peace. May He give your soul strength that you, indeed, may walk worthy of the calling to which you have been called with praise and thanksgiving! Amen.

Other Works by Fr. Jabriel

https://jahbread.com/blackpower

https://jahbread.com/championshiplove

https://jahbread.com/promisedland

www.ingramcontent.com/pod-product-compliance
Lightning Source LLC
Chambersburg PA
CBHW071531040426
42452CB00008B/965